John Heskett
born in 1937, graduated from
the London School of Economics and in 1976 was awarded
the Goldsmiths' Travelling Fellowship to study twentieth-
century German design. He is currently Associate Professor
in the Design Institute at the University of Illinois, Chicago,
and has lectured widely on his subject in Europe
and the United States.

WORLD OF ART

This famous series
provides the widest available
range of illustrated books on art in all its aspects.
If you would like to receive a complete list
of titles in print please write to:
THAMES AND HUDSON
30 Bloomsbury Street, London WC1B 3QP
In the United States please write to:
THAMES AND HUDSON INC.
500 Fifth Avenue, New York, New York 10110

Printed in Singapore

Industrial Design

JOHN HESKETT

180 illustrations

T & H

THAMES AND HUDSON

For Ingrid and Peter

Printed and bound in Singapore by C.S. Graphics

Contents

Introduction

In the last two centuries, human power to control and shape the surroundings we inhabit has been continuously augmented, to the extent that it has become a truism to speak of a man-made world. The instrument of this transformation has been mechanized industry, and from its workshops and factories a swelling flood of artefacts and mechanisms has poured out to satisfy the needs and desires of an ever-greater proportion of the world's population. The change has not only been quantitative, but has also radically altered the qualitative nature of the life we live, or aspire to live.

In the history of industrial design the twin themes of continuity and change constantly recur in different guises, and at times pronounced tensions have been created by their conflicting demands. These tensions have been reinforced by the nature of the historical evolution of industrial design. Although its roots lie in the craft tradition, the pattern of its emergence has not been simply a linear evolution from handwork to mechanical production, but, rather, a constant diversification, encompassing a broadening range of new factors and influences. A clear thread of development is discernible, however, in that design, the conception of visual form, has become progressively separated from the act of making.

In craft production, conception and realization are linked and co-ordinated by the interplay of hand, eye and materials. The fact that the entire process can be accomplished by one person disguises its complexity, giving it a human scale and apparent simplicity that allows it to be experienced by both practitioner and observer as a comprehensible unity. In mass-production industry this coherence is fragmented, and the complexity of conception and making is exposed by its subdivision into a series of specialized activities. These processes are interlinked, but in relationships that are often perceived as remote and impersonal. Despite the changed conditions of industrial production, many studies of design assume a persistence of the unity found in the craft tradition, by depicting design as an autonomous, inward-looking relationship between designer and product. The emphasis is placed on individual achievement, and the analysis of products is focused on identifying unique qualities of external form. This approach is sometimes reinforced by the practice of exhibitions and museum

7

collections, which display objects as pure forms, without reference to the circumstances of production and use that influenced their design.

This formalist methodology has been applied, not only for the analysis of the designs produced in the past, but frequently, and more questionably, to provide historical support for contemporary views on what constitutes 'good' design, usually defined in terms of specific formal principles. The emphasis, in such an approach, is generally on educating the public to accept the values and canons of taste enshrined in particular theories or institutions. By emphasizing the legitimacy of only such products as conform to these standards, it is possible to advocate the primacy or inevitability of certain traditions, thus presenting an image of formal or theoretical unity that bears little relationship to the actual diversity of design, either in the past or in the present.

In reaction against the limitations of a formalist view of ordinary objects, the profound changes wrought by industrialization have been examined by considering design as a social phenomenon. Although a valuable corrective, this approach is vulnerable to a tendency to over-emphasize the context by ignoring the individual characteristics and will of designers, and relegating their role to that of deterministic instruments of social, economic or political systems and values.

This study has drawn on both approaches, in discussing the contribution of individual designers as well as the social pressures that have moulded their work. It rejects the view that design can be assessed from a single standpoint, or in terms of a single set of values. It is based on the belief that the diversity of design requires a consideration of its varying roles and functions; and that its evaluation must be conditioned by the purposes for which it is intended, and which it actually serves. This implies a distinction between design as envisaged by a designer, and our perception of design when we observe objects in use.

In order to explain the nature of the historical evolution of industrial design, it is necessary to include discussion of the organizational and social contexts that provided the stimulus for the conception of designs, and the material and institutional frameworks that were necessary for their realization. However, this does not imply that the work of designers should be considered solely as an expression of such contextual factors: the conception of a design is not simply a representation in visual form of predetermined values, but a creative, catalytic process in which external factors interact with the beliefs, talents and skills of individual designers or design-groups. The influence of external factors is generally greatest in establishing parameters for the utilitarian function of a design – that is, the criteria by which it will be judged suitable for an intended working purpose.

Individual creativity is generally predominant in determining the extent to which the resulting form offers aesthetic experience and has a psychological or symbolic function. One of the most outstanding post-war British designers, Misha Black, affirmed the designers' own view of their role: 'That creativity is the foundation of their work, is the faith that motivates all designers . . . to exist at all as a designer, a belief in at least a modicum of personally possessed creative ability is as necessary as it is for a brick-layer to have confidence in his capability of laying a straight course of bricks.'

When manufactured, however, a design as a tangible artefact becomes part of the physical reality of its time, applied for specific purposes in a society that conditions how its form is perceived and evaluated. This evaluation may be based on premises different from those of the designer and producer, and it will be argued that the values attributed to designs in their social function are not fixed and absolute, but fluctuating and conditional.

It is plainly impossible to present in one volume even a representative selection of the multifarious range of design over a period of many decades. The text therefore seeks to survey significant general trends in the history of industrial design, and to convey the plurality of the forces and influences that have shaped its forms and characterized its social role. The specific examples discussed have, in many cases, been selected as typical of these themes and influences, rather than as uniquely representative. Although my own preferences and prejudices will be apparent, the intention in this book is not to advocate a particular viewpoint, but to stimulate an understanding of how and why the objects that surround us are as they are, and to provide an outline into which readers can interpolate their own perceptions of the objects of their daily lives.

CHAPTER ONE

From traditional crafts to industrial art

To an ever-increasing extent and across an ever-widening geographical area, our immediate visual environment is dominated by the products of industrial methods of manufacture. In the home and workplace, in schools, factories, offices and shops, in public buildings, streets and transport systems, these constitute the visible cultural landscape of everyday life, comprising in their totality a complex pattern of function and meaning, in which our perceptions of the world, our attitudes and sense of relationship to it, are closely interwoven.

Since the repetitive accuracy of machines has a precision the human hand cannot match, the shape and composition of industrial products rarely yield any indication of the participation and personality of the people who make them. For this reason, and because of their multiplicity, ubiquity and frequent complexity, they sometimes seem to assume an alien and even overpowering life of their own. They are all, however, the manifestation of a process of human design, of conception, judgment and specification, translated into tangible, material reality.

The precise nature of this process of design is infinitely varied and therefore difficult to summarize in a simple formula or definition. It can be the work of one person, or of a team working co-operatively; it may stem from a burst of creative intuition, or from a calculated judgment based on technical data or market-research investigations, or even, as some designers maintain, be determined by the taste of a managing director's wife. Constraints or opportunities may be provided by, among other factors, commercial or political decisions, the organizational context in which a designer works, the state of available material and production facilities, or prevailing social and aesthetic concepts – the range of possible permutations is immense.

Whatever the particular circumstances, however, industrial design is a process of creation, invention and definition separated from the means of production, involving an eventual synthesis of contributory and often conflicting factors into a concept of three-dimensional form, and its material reality, capable of multiple reproduction by mechanical means. It is thus specifically linked to the development of industrialization and mechanization that began with the Industrial Revolution in Britain around 1770, though it cannot be described simply as a deterministic product of those events. Its distinguishing characteristic, the separation of design from the processes of making, in fact emerged before the Industrial Revolution, with the evolution from the late medieval period onwards of early capitalist industrial organization based on craft methods of production.

The growth of trade in the medieval period was a crucial phase of this evolution towards specialization. In the burgeoning cities of Western Europe, such as Florence, Venice, Nuremberg and Bruges, large workshops developed to cater for the sophisticated tastes of courts, churches and rich merchants. Though traditional skills and techniques still predominated, they became more specialized. Many objects of the same type were made, though the process of production was essentially the repetitive duplication of existing models by craft methods. Much work produced by these urban craftsmen was of a high level of skill and artistry, and the boundaries between artist and craftsmen were fluid, depending upon degree of achievement based on a common training and technique, rather than on differences in the nature and type of activity.

The continuing expansion of trade and commercial opportunities, however, and the growth in size of production units, created competitive pressures that in turn led to demand for innovation, and for some characteristic feature or aspect of skill to distinguish a product and attract the interest of customers. In the early sixteenth century, in Italy and Germany, the first, nascent designers began to cater for that need with pattern books. These books were collections of engravings produced in quantity by new mechanical printing methods, illustrating decorative forms, patterns and motifs, and generally intended for such textile trades as ribbon-making, or for cabinet-making. The pattern books contained designs that could be applied repetitively and in a variety of contexts, and their significance for the history of industrial design was that a designer, by publishing in this form, was divorced from any involvement in the means by which the patterns were applied and used.

In the seventeenth century, as the centre of trade in Europe shifted from the Mediterranean region to the Atlantic seaboard, the focal points of power became nation-states under centralized, monarchical governments, epitomized by the France of Louis XIV. During the reign of the 'Sun King', the scale and grandeur of court life provided lavish patronage for artists and skilled craftsmen, culminating in the establishment of manufactories financed and controlled by the Crown. The most famous of these, founded in 1667, was at Gobelins, which although best known for its tapestries, also provided facilities for cabinet-makers and craftsmen in fine metals. It was a large-scale operation, the number of craftsmen running into hundreds, with a school for sixty apprentices. Designs were provided by Charles Le Brun, premier artist to Louis XIV and director of the Gobelins manufactory, and a staff of artists, decorators and engravers, for a range of articles such as coaches, tapestries and furniture, often so sumptuously decorated that one hesitates to refer to them as utilitarian.

Other monarchs of states both large and small attempted to emulate the pattern of absolutist government and the grand style of French court life. The concentration of power at the centre was followed by the spread of mercantilist economic principles, harnessing and controlling resources, skills and products for the purposes and profit of the state, embodied in the person of the ruler. Consequently, artistic patronage and royal investment went hand in hand, most notably in the great porcelain manufactories founded throughout Europe in the eighteenth century.

The delicate porcelain imported from China in the seventeenth century was superior in structure to any ceramic product in Europe, and had such appeal in court circles that it stimulated a wave of research to discover the secrets of its production, the key breakthrough being achieved in 1709 at the Meissen manufactory established by the Grand Duke of Saxony. The approach to design at Meissen was typical in drawing on a variety of sources. Initially, the readily available skills of court artists and craftsmen, such as the goldsmith Johann Jakob Irminger, were extended to designs for vessels, figures and decorative motifs; and by the mid-1720s, academically trained sculptors were also employed to model the figurines for which Meissen became famous. In addition, many designs originated from anonymous craftsmen employed in the manufactory. A further major source of designs was pattern books, which continued to be published in considerable quantities. In the 1720s Meissen produced a series known as 'Callot figures', based on a volume of engravings by Jacques Callot published in Amsterdam in 1716. Such volumes provided a ready source of reference for figure-models, decorative motifs and details, and their influence was at times remarkably widespread.

Porcelain was initially produced as an adjunct to court life; consequently, the emphasis in design was on artistic quality and exquisite craftsmanship, irrespective of cost. The massive subsidies required to support the manufactories, however, were a heavy financial burden, and by the mid-eighteenth century new commercial markets were being broached to offset some of the operating costs. The newly acquired tastes for tea, coffee and cocoa among the growing middle classes led to an extension of the use of porcelain, and a change of emphasis in design from artistic exclusivity to commercial acceptability. Some manufactories also became heavily involved in export markets, Meissen, for example, coming to dominate the Turkish trade in handleless coffee cups. The expansion was generally met by an extension of craft methods, and the artistic quality of work inevitably deteriorated under the pressures of large-scale production.

Although design in Europe was predominantly for the products of royal manufactories, by the second half of the eighteenth century it had also become established in France as a specialist, and often highly paid, activity in commercial companies dependent upon good-quality surface-pattern design, such as textiles and wallpaper manufactories. And with the collapse of the absolutist system of government under the impact of the French Revolution, such former royal manufactories as survived had to adapt to commercial competition, their designers becoming independent employees instead of court functionaries.

In many respects, the factors influencing design in Britain in the eighteenth century were little different from those prevailing in Europe. It was a rich period for pattern books, many leading artists providing designs for a great variety of objects. A major difference, however, was that the continental form of absolute monarchy had failed to establish itself in Britain, and the economic values of commercial freedom and private profit were furthered and staunchly defended by Parliament, in which, as Eric Hobsbawn aptly put it, 'money not only talked, but governed'. This explains why so many of the famous names most closely identified with the designs and products of this period were not artists and designers, but commercial entrepreneurs and innovators such as Chippendale, Wedgwood and Boulton.

Typical were the developments that took place in the production of what were known as 'toys' – the staples of the Birmingham metal trades, such as buttons, buckles, clasps and mounts. In the mid-eighteenth century, manufacture was still based on traditional methods and a network of small workshops, though a high degree of specialization existed in the various stages of production. Matthew Boulton, who inherited his father's business in 1759, set out to meet the fierce competition in the toy trade, and produce more cheaply than his rivals, by introducing a larger scale of production based on mechanized means of manufacture. A site was therefore purchased for a factory at Soho in 1761, suitable for the erection of large workshops and adjacent to a stream for water-powered machinery. Production was expanded, and by the time the Soho Foundry was completed in 1766, more than six hundred men were employed.

The main output continued to be competitively priced fashionable objects for what, at the time, was a mass market, but Boulton soon began to expand into new areas of manufacture, such as Sheffield Plate, an inexpensive *2* method of plating silver to a copper base, which later led to the production of solid silver plate, and ormolu, an amalgam of ground gold and mercury

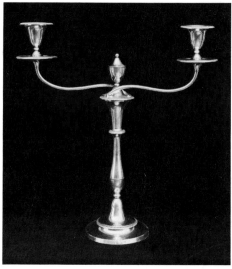

1–2 The feathery rococo decoration of a pair of ewers in Derbyshire fluorspar and ormolu (left) and the restrained Neo-classical elegance of a Sheffield Plate candelabra (right) demonstrate the range of both materials and styles that characterized Matthew Boulton's designs at all levels of production

1 used to gild brass mouldings. Numerous other ideas and ventures were attempted, some successful, others financially near-catastrophic. Indeed, Boulton often appeared to court commercial disaster with the spread of products that emerged from Soho, some mass-produced for a volatile market, others utilizing expensive materials and a high level of craft skill, and obviously intended for a more discerning clientele. There was a logic to this diversity, however, and design was a key factor.

Boulton's approach to design was eclectic, a mirror of prevailing contemporary attitudes. 'Fashion hath much to do in these things,' he wrote, 'and that of the present age distinguishes itself by adopting the most Elegant ornaments without presuming to invent new ones.' Eclecticism, as well as cheapness, was therefore a commercial imperative, the fashionable market requiring a wide range of choice; and since Boulton's goods were also sold internationally, close attention was paid to the differing needs and variations of taste in specific markets. The pattern books collated at Soho included forms derived from a multiplicity of sources, Boulton frequently borrowing works from friends and acquaintances so that casts and drawings could be made. His network of agents at home and abroad also supplied a stream of objects, casts, books and sketches, and, in addition, models and drawings were purchased from prominent artists such as John Flaxman and James

Wyatt. Although little is known about the draughtsmen and skilled workers at Soho, it would seem that the majority of Boulton's designs were devised by them using forms and models collected from elsewhere, rather than obtained by external commissions.

The best work produced by Boulton was in the Neo-classical style 2 inspired by Robert and James Adam, which became the dominant taste among the aristocracy and middle classes of the late eighteenth century. The extent to which the Adam brothers actually designed for Boulton is uncertain, but their indirect influence on his products was undoubtedly considerable, and the conjunction of commercial opportunity and the Neo-classical fashion was especially fortunate. The style's basic geometrical simplicity and repetitive use of classical motifs made it ideally suited to multiple reproduction, and Boulton's exploitation of these features was the vital link between mass-production and craftwork at Soho.

His policy was to build up a staff of highly skilled craftsmen who could maintain standards in the mass-production sector and also apply their talents to the more demanding but irregular production of quality wares. Basic designs and components could be applied across the range, the moulds and dies being adaptable to different metals. But although the methods were industrial, the element of individual skill was still essential, the amount of hand-finishing and craftsmanship lavished on the finer wares setting them on a level apart. Such luxury goods were not particularly profitable, but brought Boulton a reputation for quality and a large number of acquaintances in leading artistic and social circles, and the constant flow of ideas and designs obtained through these contacts in turn benefited the lucrative mass-production sector.

A similar relationship between different categories of products existed in the structure of the pottery firm built up by Boulton's contemporary and close acquaintance, Josiah Wedgwood, though it was made more explicit here by a clear organizational division into what were termed respectively 'useful' and 'ornamental' wares. Like Boulton's luxury production, Wedgwood's finest ornamental ware was in the prevailing Neo-classical style, and of fine materials, especially the Basalt and Jasper bodies. Prominent artists such as John Flaxman, George Stubbs and Joseph Wright were commissioned for designs, which, although utilizing mechanical devices such as lathes, required a high degree of skill in their execution and finishing. The artistic success of Wedgwood's ornamental ware was enormous, gaining him an international reputation as the outstanding figure in the field of ceramic production of his time.

That reputation was undoubtedly deserved, but needs to be set in the context of Wedgwood's total achievement. As with Boulton, the volume-

3 Wedgwood's ideal of 'elegance and simplicity' is epitomized by the graceful proportions of a dinner-set in Queen's Ware, *c.* 1790, decorated with the 'Green Water Leaf' pattern

production of useful ware provided the human, technical and financial resources without which the more irregular and demanding production of ornamental ware would not have been possible. The useful ware, however, is worthy of attention in its own right.

The North Staffordshire pottery industry was still small-scale in the mid-eighteenth century, but two strands of innovation lifted it above the level of a country craft. One was a series of attempts to simulate the whiteness of porcelain by washes and improved mixtures of clay; the other, the development of methods of repetitively casting liquid clay in moulds, instead of throwing individual pieces and shaping them by hand on a wheel. Wedgwood's work can be seen as continuing and uniting these two trends. His experiments to improve materials, however, were directed, not towards the imitation of porcelain, but to refining the unique features of traditional materials. One of the earliest fruits of this approach, developed by a series of rigorous and exhaustive investigations over several years, was the cream earthenware later known as 'Queen's Ware', first produced in 1763. Wedgwood described it as 'a species of earthenware for the table, quite new in appearance . . . manufactured with ease and expedition, and consequently

3

cheap'. There is more than a touch of modest understatement in that description. Queen's Ware was revolutionary, its quality and suitability for casting opening the era of modern ceramics production. Wedgwood was not only an outstanding experimental scientist, but also a perceptive entrepreneur who realized that a large potential market existed for good, inexpensive tableware. The factory he built at Etruria was planned for the application of mechanical appliances, division of labour, and, by the standards of the time, high volume-production requiring intensive marketing. Catalogues were printed to advertise his wares, commencing in 1773, and six editions of the 'Useful Ware' catalogue were published, with French, German and Dutch editions.

These innovations had a radical effect on the process of design. The precision of repetitive moulding removed control over the form from the executant workers, placing the whole responsibility for quality on the prototype designs. Skilled modellers and designers were at a premium, and by 1775 Wedgwood had seven in full-time employment, working across the product-range. The volume-production of useful ware also demanded a more rapid method of decoration than hand-painting, though the latter was still used for special orders of table services. Techniques of printing transfers for ceramic decoration had been developed by the firm of Sadler and Green of Liverpool in 1752, and they were engaged by Wedgwood to produce patterns to his specification. In addition, pattern books were compiled containing designs for borders and decorative motifs, and shape books with drawings of forms and specification of sizes.

Reviewing the state of the industry in his early working years, Wedgwood once wrote: 'with regard to Elegance of form, that was an object very little attended to'. He later frequently described his own ideal as 'elegance and simplicity'. Some of his early useful ware, from around 1760, 4
hardly matched this ideal, being moulded in a variety of fruit- and

4 A Wedgwood coffee-pot of *c*. 1760 in a cauliflower pattern was typical of the fashion for fruit- and vegetable-shapes in ceramics that predominated in the mid-eighteenth century

vegetable-shapes, in the then-current rococo taste. The enthusiasm with which Wedgwood embraced the Neo-classical fashion seemed, however, to be due to personal inclination as much as commercial instinct. It was a felicitous combination of traditional, functional forms for domestic use, evolved in North Staffordshire, and the 'elegance and simplicity' manifested in the Neo-classical ornamental ware, that was to be the supreme achievement of Wedgwood's useful ware.

There were several features of Boulton's and Wedgwood's firms that presaged future developments. Comparing the two, an essential difference emerges between their respective types of volume-production. Boulton's was of decorative products for a fashionable market of rapid changes in taste; Wedgwood's was of domestic objects in which aesthetic form had to be reconciled with requirements of utility and durability. These two broad categories of consumption, with their differing implications for design, emerged ever more strongly as industrialization spread. Two other significant features were common to both firms. First, although aesthetic values were important, they were subordinate to questions of commercial viability, the dominant criterion for products being: would they sell? Secondly, in each case the sources of designs were predominantly from outside the firms, from artists, architects and publications providing forms, patterns and motifs in circumstances divorced from the production process. Designs were applied to the process, and not, in most cases, derived from it. This breach could be overcome given the modest scale and essential unity of each of the two firms, but became more problematic as production units increased in size, complexity and degree of specialization.

It was in nineteenth-century Britain as the Industrial Revolution gathered momentum that the gulf between design and production became most acute. Here it should be pointed out that the process of industrialization does not always involve fundamental changes in production technology. If in some industries, such as textiles, mechanization resulted, bringing changes that were indeed dramatic, in others, larger units were formed but production techniques remained based on handwork. The furniture industry, for example, developed numerous large firms, but did not introduce mechanization on a large scale until the twentieth century. In some industries, the tradition of small craft businesses continued to predominate, while these became more specialized and diversified, like the independent craftsmen known as the 'Little Mesters' of the Sheffield cutlery and metalware trades. The gun and jewellery trades of Birmingham were similar, located in a quarter of the city that was a warren of small specialist workshops. The common factor in all these different forms of organization was not mechanization, but the commercialization of production.

Discussion of design in nineteenth-century Britain was dominated by the tension created between a continuing and expanding demand for articles with a tradition of craft production, such as furniture, ceramics and metalwares, and the development of a commercialized production which appropriated and modified the forms and values of the past, making them accessible to a greater proportion of the population.

Traditionally, ornament and decoration were an expression of craftsmen's skill and virtuosity in working precious and delicate materials, a visible indication of economic and aesthetic value. With the introduction of large-scale commercial production, however, objects and artefacts could readily be produced in new materials such as cast iron, papier mâché and gutta percha, using new techniques of stamping, moulding, plating and veneering, to simulate both precious materials and skilled craftsmanship. Rich textures and intricate design, formerly a sign of quality and exclusivity, thus became widely accessible at modest cost. Such products met with ready acceptance among the new middle classes, who demanded public and domestic environments that would proclaim their taste and standing, and whose newly acquired wealth and position often manifested itself in a piling-up of decorative effect, resulting in an exuberant and florid vulgarity. Equally, a temptation existed for manufacturers seeking profitability to use decoration to make simple articles look more complex, and therefore more expensive, than they needed to be. While academic research and intellectual debate were directed to determining which historical form was most suitable for adoption as á contemporary national style, manufacturers pillaged the stylistic canons of past cultures in search of novelty. Consequently, the indiscriminate application of ornament resulted all too often in a gulf between style and function. A lack of trained designers exacerbated the situation, and was satirized in mock advertisements on the title page of A. N. W. Pugin's *Contrasts*, published in 1836, which included, 'Designing taught in six lessons, Gothic, Severe Greek and mixed styles', and, 'An Errand Boy for an Office who can design occasionally'. In a later book, *The True Principles of Pointed or Christian Architecture*, Pugin vehemently denounced 'the false notion of disguising instead of beautifying articles of utility'. The remedy he proposed for current ills, however, was deeply coloured by his devout Catholicism, requiring a return to the faith of the Middle Ages as the only means of attaining beauty and fitness in architecture and design.

The most profoundly influential criticism was that of John Ruskin, William Morris and their followers, who shared Pugin's admiration of medieval society and art, but expanded his equation of aesthetic and ethical values in their sweeping condemnation of industry and its products, pointing to the human cost and sacrifice involved in a social system that required and produced such goods. They did much to arouse the conscience of Victorian Britain and had a great impact abroad, but the influence of their ideas on industry was limited, these being based essentially on a nostalgia for the craft culture of the past, rather than on efforts to recognize and improve the situation as it existed.

The conviction that improvement could be effected by aesthetic means produced several practical proposals. Belief in the educative value of art, based on the hierarchical concept that if the higher or fine arts flourished, so too would the lesser or applied arts, resulted in a wave of proposals to improve art education and establish museums and collections freely available to the public. Some people, however, attempted to come to terms with industry more directly. Chief among these in the mid-nineteenth century was Henry Cole, a civil servant who was one of the driving forces behind the realization of the plans for the Great Exhibition of 1851. In 1849 he founded the *Journal of Design*, edited by Richard Redgrave, which for three years served as a vehicle for the propagation and elaboration of his ideas. Cole and his colleagues shared many attitudes with contemporary critics regarding the moral value of art and the importance of ornament, but differed in their belief that practical reform was possible by reconciling artistic values with utility and commercial production. In an early issue of the *Journal* an editorial stated: 'Design has a twofold relation, having in the first place, a strict reference to utility in the thing designed; and, secondarily, to the beautifying or ornamenting that utility. The word *design*, however, with the many has become identified rather with its secondary than with its whole signification – with ornament, as apart from, and often even as opposed to, utility. From thus confounding that which is in itself but an addition, with that which is essential, has arisen many of those great errors in *taste* which are observable in the works of modern designers.'

The root of the problem was correctly identified as the separation of design from the processes of production. A later article referred to this point

5 A copper coal-scuttle by Tylers of London illustrated in the *Journal of Design* of 1849

6 Two designs for candlesticks
by Sturges of Birmingham from
the *Journal of Design*, 1850

more specifically: 'the acme of beauty in design is only to be attained, when the system of ornamentation is conducted in strict accordance with the scientific theory of production – when, in fact, the physical condition of materials, and the economic processes of manufacture, limit and dictate the boundaries within which the imagination of the designer may revel.'

The six volumes of the *Journal* displayed a wide range of work that demonstrated Cole's ideas. Some of the pieces were simple objects, like a copper coal-scuttle by Tylers of London, its curved shape commended for ease of use, and for the relationship of its form to function, with the comment: 'This is an illustration of the improvement every object gains, even in the condition of beauty of line, by being first of all thoroughly well adapted to its purpose.' The emphasis on the aesthetic value of utilitarian form was somewhat atypical, however. The majority of examples were more decorative, and the discussion focused on the appropriateness of the ornament, as with two designs for candlesticks by Sturges of Birmingham. The comments on these objects accepted cheapness as an advantage, the overriding concern being that the decoration should be 'properly controlled'. Ornament was not simply regarded as an addition, but had a necessity of its own. This was articulated in a lecture by William Dyce that the *Journal* published: 'ornamental art is an ingredient necessary to the completeness of the results of mechanical skill. I say necessary, because we all feel it to be so. The love of ornament is a tendency of our being. We all are sensible, and we cannot help being so, that mechanical contrivances are like skeletons without skin, like birds without feathers – pieces of organization, in short, without the ingredient which renders natural productions objects of

7 Italian warm-air stove of cast bronze with panels of earthenware by Minton. Designed by Alfred Stevens for Hoole of Sheffield and shown at the Great Exhibition of 1851

pleasure to the senses.' Although utility was constantly emphasized, ornament was also accepted as an integral function. The problem was to establish harmony between the two.

The realization of these ideas and an improvement in design was not contingent on manufacturers' and designers' efforts only; the *Journal* stressed that the public has a responsibility. 'If the public are unable to appreciate excellence, surely we cannot call on the manufacturer to produce it at a sacrifice?' This realistic understanding of the manufacturers' position was a marked exception in contemporary criticism, as was the decision that each month the *Journal* would discuss '*selected specimens of successful decorative manufactures, considered with reference to the use of them by the consumer*'. That the point of departure should be consumer-use instead of elevated standards of artistic taste was a considerable innovation.

There were artists, too, who attempted to come to terms with the problems of designing for industry. Alfred Stevens, a sculptor, was commissioned by several firms in Sheffield while living there between 1849 and 1852, most notably by Hoole and Co., specialists in cast-iron ovens and fire-grates. His design for the 'Proserpine' fire-place was an outstanding 8 example of his approach, with restrained and finely detailed ornament, incorporating technical innovations to increase efficiency and reduce heat-loss. The warm-air stove designed as the centre-piece of Hoole's exhibit at 7 the Great Exhibition showed a similar concern to reconcile ornament and utility: its perforated foliage-patterns clearly demonstrated the high

8 The 'Proserpine' fire-place by Alfred Stevens for Hoole of Sheffield, 1850

standards of casting for which the firm was renowned, and acted as vents for heat emission. Co-operation between artists and industry was not easily achieved, however, as many anecdotes about Stevens' experiences reveal. He had a deep belief in the capacity of workers' skill and ability to contribute creatively to higher standards, and on one occasion set about teaching workers in Hoole's casting shop a new technique that he considered essential for the realization of one of his designs. Henry Hoole, on hearing of this, escorted him from the premises with the tart comment that Stevens was not employed to educate the work-force.

However, other employers, less obdurate than Hoole, saw education and staff training as a means of improving their standards of design. Elkingtons of Birmingham released over fifty assistants for classes in design at the Midland Institute in the city, while Henry Doulton, after employing some students in his pottery firm on an experimental basis, established the Lambeth Studio that grew to employ over two hundred, serving as a model for other companies' design studios.

9, 10   An outstanding illustration of the possibilities of reconciling commercial and aesthetic values was provided by Christopher Dresser, who began his career as a teacher of botany after studying at the School of Design in London. There, he was deeply influenced by the teachings of Owen Jones, a close colleague of Henry Cole, who sought to formulate rules governing

9–10 The freshness and originality of Christopher Dresser's forms is manifested in two contrasting materials: a glass claret jug of 1882 for Hukin & Heath of Birmingham (left); and a silver tea-set of 1880 for James Dixon of Sheffield (above right)

design that would make it an expression of the needs and sentiments of the age. Jones' ideas, published as the 'Grammar of Ornament', were based on studies of the structure of natural forms, and of past styles, though emphasizing their underlying principles rather than their results. He accepted the importance of function, arguing for its integration with 'an imaginative and intelligent eclecticism' in adapting past forms to present needs. Dresser was to go further than his mentor, his analysis of the geometry and structural principles of natural forms leading to a rejection of representation and stylistic solutions.

Around 1860, after approaches from several manufacturers with commissions, Dresser abandoned botany in order to concentrate on design, and until his death in 1904 was fully engaged with work in both two and three dimensions. Among his most outstanding achievements was a series of metalware designs for three firms: James Dixon of Sheffield, and Hukin & *10* Heath and Elkingtons of Birmingham. Dresser's elegant geometric forms owed little to historical precedent, and were characterized by a simplicity based on a meticulous analysis of function, paying close attention to ease of manufacture and use. His designs derived their aesthetic quality from an enhancement of the materials used, rather than stylistic references, and his originality was revealed in a continual variety and inventiveness that never lapsed into a repetitive pattern. His awareness of the commercial context in which his work was produced was clear in the stress he placed on economy of materials to reduce costs, in order, as he stated, that products might not be placed 'beyond the reach of those who might otherwise enjoy them'.

Dresser's work and writings, and his understanding of the skill and craftsmanship of the metal-workers in the firms for which he designed, exemplified the possibilities of a renewal of traditional values and techniques. His recognition of the changed circumstances and opportunities provided by industrialization, grounded in a strong enthusiasm for the age in which he lived and a belief in its potential, represented an embryonic, positive point of departure for future development. Yet despite such attempts to effect improvement by adapting to changed conditions of production and use, it was the power of tradition embodied in the anti-industrial doctrines of Ruskin, Morris and the Arts and Crafts Movement that dominated attitudes to design in Britain, even though their reaction to the age in which they lived was essentially negative. Industrial design lacked an advocate of the stature of Ruskin, who, in his lectures and writings, hammered home his ideas with force, prophetic conviction and majestic oratory. In an article 'The Cestus of Aglaia', published in *The Art Journal* of 1865, he posed the question: '. . . how far . . . the Fine Arts may advisably supersede or regulate the mechanical arts?' The terms in which the question was framed left little doubt about his answer. Although he confessed to 'the amazed awe, the crushed humility – with which I sometimes watch a locomotive take its breath at a railway station', admiring its precision and mechanical finesse, the products of the 'mechanical art' clearly had no place in his aesthetic philosophy. 'For after all,' he dismissively concluded, 'this shrieking thing, whatever the fine make of it may be, can but pull, or push, and do oxen's work, in an impetuous manner.'

In his total denial of the possibility that industrial products might have aesthetic value, Ruskin epitomized the strong element of social and intellectual rigidity in Britain that rejected the sweeping implications of the prodigy it had spawned. The problems of the age were identified with great clarity and passion, but the innate conservatism that dominated the artistic life and aesthetic vision of the country prevented any real recognition of the achievement and potential of industry, leading instead to a retreat into a nostalgic image of the past. Meanwhile, the visual environment and the life of its inhabitants were being transformed at every level by the products of factories and workshops. To decry their validity might bring temporary comfort, but they could not be permanently ignored.

CHAPTER TWO

Industrialization and the search for harmony

The Industrial Revolution not only transformed traditional crafts, but, as the pace of technical innovation increased, established many new industries which applied mechanized processes to the production of a host of new forms. If such industrial products were excluded from aesthetic consideration when judged by the canons of traditionally oriented artistic philosophies, there were engineers and designers in the new industries who were equally adamant in rejecting aesthetic influences and denying them any role in their work. Typical of this view was Zarah Colburn, a civil engineer who wrote a treatise intended for the general public in 1871 entitled, *Locomotive Engineering and the Mechanism of Railways*. Colburn's standpoint was unequivocally utilitarian: 'Commercial results are now the chief object of Engineering, and the Author has no sympathy with that affectation which would exclude the consideration of such results.' On the subject of aesthetics he was scornful, insisting that 'none who aspire to become engineers should encourage any play of imagination involving the forms or proportions of mere mechanism, but . . . should apply themselves solely to the consideration of the best mechanical means by which any mechanical purpose under consideration may be accomplished.'

In contrast to the irreconcilable extremes of aesthetic and utilitarian particularism, the writings of the German architect Gottfried Semper defined an aesthetic theory which accepted the inevitability of industrialization and confronted the problems of the interrelationship between art and industry.

A refugee after the collapse of the 1848 Revolution in Prussia, Semper lived in London from 1851 until 1854. Unable to practise as an architect in this period, he turned to the applied arts, in which he had long been interested, teaching at the School of Design, and coming into contact with Henry Cole and his circle. In 1852 he published a pamphlet entitled *Wissenschaft, Industrie und Kunst* (Science, Industry and Art), based on his impressions of the Great Exhibition of the previous year. Like many other observers he was critical of the exhibits, but concluded that the problem lay in coming to terms with scientific and technical advance. He acknowledged the divorce between art and industry, but argued that the legacy of the past, and specifically craft traditions, had to be swept away before it would be

27

possible to create a new art, based on an acceptance and command of mechanization. 'I do not deplore the general situation,' he wrote; 'I am sure that sooner or later there will be a change to the benefit and honour of society in every way.'

His theories were based on an extensive study of history, particularly of the applied arts and their techniques. This led him to conclude, in contrast to contemporary academic scholarship, that style was not an amalgam of the forms characteristic of a period, but 'the elevation to artistic significance of the content of the basic idea' in designing an artefact. This concept of basic form, he argued, was modified primarily by the materials and processes employed upon it, and also by 'many influences outside the work itself, which are important factors contributing to its design', including location, climate, time, custom, and the position of the person for whom the work is intended. Decoration as an expression of these influences was thus an integral element.

His writings revealed an enormous breadth of learning, and were to have a profound, if belated, influence in the early twentieth century, when a reaction set in against stylistic revivalism and ornamentation. In the search for aesthetic forms and a rationale that would more adequately correspond to and be expressive of the technological nature of the modern world, many designers turned to the machines, instruments and products of industry as exemplars of their theories. By the 1920s a 'machine aesthetic' had emerged, emphasizing abstract, geometric forms linked to a philosophy of functionalism.

In the search for precedents and justifications for these functionalist ideas, Semper's works became an important source, particularly his principle of basic form. This was adapted to a historical interpretation of a vernacular tradition, that in contrast to the decorative arts, accepted and utilized machines to produce timeless, functional forms of geometric simplicity. It was an essentially teleological approach to design history, selecting and appropriating suitable examples from the past to incorporate into a tradition confirming and substantiating the contemporary 'machine aesthetic'.

The functionalist interpretation could be partially sustained by the fact that some machines and products manufactured in the nineteenth century were indeed unadorned and geometric, deriving their form from structure and mechanical function. The progress of industrial technology hinged upon developing finer tolerances and accuracy, in which mathematics was a basic tool, and geometry provided the three-dimensional form in which the necessary precision could be attained. Despite the imperatives of mechanical function and serviceability, however, there still remained open possibilities in the disposition and arrangement of forms, providing opportunities for

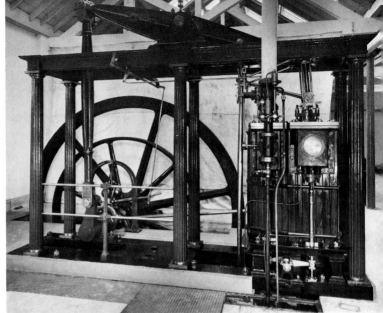

11 The static formality of the Neo-classical elements used to frame the Amos beam engine of 1867 symbolized the scientific rationality and order of the principles embodied in the engine rather than the dynamics of its movement when operating

aesthetic judgments, and even decoration. The frequent use of cast-iron classical columns to support the frames of early static steam engines, for *11* example, can hardly be justified as an inevitable expression of mechanical function. They were based rather on a belief in the appropriateness of that particular stylistic form, with its geometric emphasis, as a decorative device.

It is therefore ironic that when Semper's ideas found acceptance they were applied to a search for universal forms that ignored the most essential and relevant quality of his understanding of history: the recognition that designs were a response to the specific needs that gave rise to them, and particular to the time, place and social conditions in which they were produced.

If nineteenth-century design is considered as a whole in the light of this crucial aspect of Semper's thought, it becomes clear that a vast body of work was created in many industries that rejected the polarization of aesthetic and utilitarian values, seeking instead to reconcile and unify them.

The development of railways provides a key example of the evolution of design in relation to the new technology. The spread of railways across every country and continent was responsible, more than anything else, for the transformation of nineteenth-century work and life. Great new industries were established to construct the locomotives, rolling stock, and apparatus of an enormous range and diversity essential to their operation. In many respects they were designed in a situation of compulsory originality, there being simply no available precedents. But not all areas of production were uniquely innovative; some still depended upon the adaptation of traditional

29

12 The *Wylam Dilly* built by Christopher Blackett in 1813 for use at Wylam Colliery in County Durham typifies the unembellished forms of locomotives at a point where they first became a functional reality

techniques, a contrast best exemplified by a comparison of the respective designs for locomotives and railway carriages.

The earliest locomotives were somewhat primitive experiments, the main purpose being to develop the mechanism as a functioning instrument. Their construction and technology was within the capacity of local carpenters and 12 blacksmiths, and their appearance reflected their reality. The *Wylam Dilly* built by Christopher Blackett for William Hedley in 1813, for use at Wylam Colliery near Newcastle, looks what it is, a scaled-down beam engine on wheels, whose form directly reflected mechanical function. By 1829, on the occasion of the Rainhill Trials, a competition to select locomotives for use on the world's first regular steam-hauled passenger services between Liverpool and Manchester, a much greater degree of assurance was apparent in both the efficient performance and the appearance of the winner, George 13 Stephenson's *Rocket*. This engine embodied all the basic technical features later extended and developed in locomotive design, but although it had a neatness that set it apart from its competitors and predecessors, to speak of an 'aesthetic' treatment would be inappropriate. It was a different matter with 14 the *Jenny Lind*, designed by David Joy in 1847 for the London, Brighton and South Coast Railway. The railways' rapid development in the two intervening decades was reflected in its size and structure. The days of local jobbing craftsmen and timber frames were past; engineering construction

30

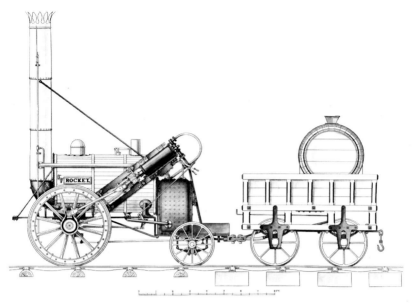

13 The *Rocket* of 1829 built by George and Robert Stephenson, father and son, with
Henry Booth. Robert Stephenson was primarily responsible for a design that was a
notable mechanical advance, though little attention was paid to formal composition

14 The *Jenny Lind* of 1847, designed by David Joy for the London, Brighton and
South Coast Railway. In both overall proportions and detailing the emergence of a
conscious aesthetic treatment of locomotives is apparent

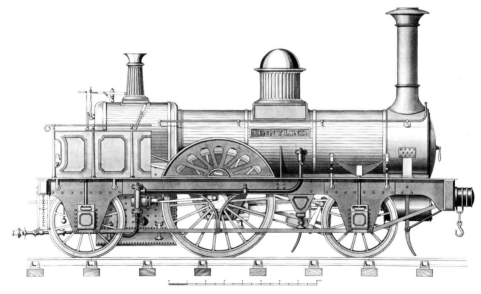

was clearly emerging as a technological discipline in its own right, and a significant advance was the attention paid to appearance. The metal frame provided an extended horizontal unifying feature echoed by the line of the boiler. The classical columnar and dome forms of the safety-valve and steam-dome were pure aesthetic choices, and the driving-wheel splasher with its fretted wall and the panelling of the cab were carefully detailed. The placing of the cylinders and driving-motion inside the frame, although having a technical rationale, was also justified in producing clean, uncluttered lines.

The method of construction contributed incidentally to the visual appeal of such locomotives; although many examples of a particular engine might be constructed, each was built individually, and the amount of handwork and hand-finishing gave a quality of detail that enables one to speak of a new type of industrial craftsman.

The intense competition between rival railway companies in nineteenth-century Britain reinforced the emphasis on appearance. Each company developed a particular style in design, intended to create a completely different visual ambience. This distinctiveness extended beyond the forms of locomotive and carriages to liveries and colour-schemes, uniforms for staff, publications and fixtures and fittings of all kinds; a forerunner, in fact, of modern corporate identity programmes.

By the late nineteenth century, locomotive design had not only achieved new heights of performance and efficiency, but also strove for an aesthetic perfection that would be a mobile advertisement for the operating company. 15 Typical was Samuel Johnson's 4–4–0 *1562* express locomotive design of 1893 for the Midland Railway. In his youth, Johnson had been apprenticed to the firm of E. B. Wilson at the Leeds Engine Foundry where the *Jenny Lind* had been built, and had assisted David Joy in preparing the drawings for that engine. His 1893 design also had inside cylinders, concentrating attention on an uncluttered external outline. The result was a beautifully proportioned design, with each element harmonized into a coherent whole. Although the chimney, dome and safety-valve casings were of different shapes and sizes, they were symmetrically balanced in relation to one another, an unseen line of diminishing height connecting the top of all three to the roof of the cab. The curves at the base of all three, and of the boiler, the emphatic flow of the splashers over the driving wheels and the arc of the cab, integrated one part into another. With a livery of dark crimson-lake and polished brass fittings, it was one of the most elegant locomotives of its time, built to a high standard of workmanship, and excellent in performance.

The steam engine thus developed in nineteenth-century Britain from a crude mechanism to a sophisticated and efficient form of locomotion,

32

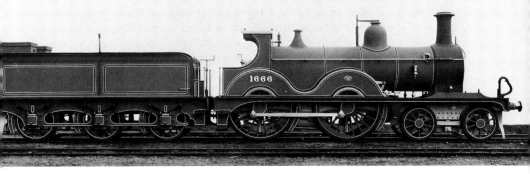

15 Number *1666* of Samuel Johnson's *1562* class of 4–4–0 express locomotives for the Midland Railway, 1893. The assured symmetry and clean flowing lines are characteristic of British locomotive design in the late nineteenth century

combining technical efficiency and aesthetic expression. In some respects it is surprising that so much locomotive design was so good. The process of design was not only separated from production physically, but socially as well: workers in the drawing office were considered to have professional status, while those in the foundries and erection shops were artisans. Locomotive design was also a co-operative process, with a large team of technical specialists, draughtsmen and clerical staff – the days were long past when one man could assume total responsibility for a design. However, two important factors contributed to the effectiveness of this organizational structure. First, engineers and designers generally went through a process of apprenticeship on the shop-floor which, to judge by one engineer's recollections of his youthful experiences with the Lancashire and Yorkshire Railway in the 1890s, maintained the spirit of the traditional crafts: 'Nobody received more than a few minutes' instruction at a time from leading hand or mate. Turning on the lathe, and later, chipping and filing on the fitting bench had to be picked up by observation, trial and error, and the application of such mother wit as one might possess. But what one learnt in this rough and ready way was remembered and one picked up a lot of the art of dealing with human beings in the process.' The British railway industry was a closed world in which one generally made a career for life, so that designers' and engineers' practical grounding was applied, and ensured that whatever the possibilities of aesthetic expression, they were not imposed as an external factor, but had to be reconciled to functional demands. Secondly, the companies were structured on a pattern derived from military forms of organization. The design process might indeed involve many people, but

33

there was a distinct hierarchy in which everyone's role and work were clearly defined. The Locomotive Superintendent could not design every detail personally, but he established the framework, had the final word, and bore the overall responsibility.

Locomotive design had no precedents, and its forms were unique products of their time. The same cannot be said of carriage design, which, in its origins and functions, displayed very different characteristics. The first railway carriages in Britain were simply stage-coaches set on a railway truck. The speed with which the railways supplanted the stage-coach probably accelerated the flight of coachbuilders to railway construction-shops as their traditional livelihood became threatened. Perhaps, too, passengers venturing on this strange mode of transport needed the security of familiar forms. For whatever reasons, the forms and techniques of British railway-carriage design remained firmly in the hands of coachbuilders until the twentieth century. The early method of adaptation was to mount stage-coach bodies end to end on an elongated chassis, so that they formed separate compartments with side doors. Carriages for the first-class passengers were well upholstered, the forms and fittings mirroring contemporary domestic tastes, and were tolerably comfortable, despite a lack of lighting, heating and toilet facilities. In the second-class coaches the latter deficiencies were compounded by hard wooden bench-seats. Even these were luxurious, however, compared to the low-sided carriages, open to the elements, that were the lot of third-class passengers. In Europe the pattern was at first

16 The *Traveller* coach of the Liverpool and Manchester Railway from the early 1830s clearly has its origins in stage-coach design. The third-class open carriage, left, was based on traditional cart forms. Passengers were not only open to the elements but also to smoke and cinders from the engine

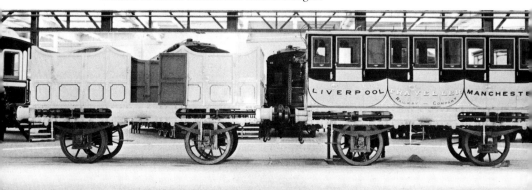

17–18 The open-plan Baltimore and Ohio Railroad car of the mid-1860s (left) epitomizes the design of American passenger cars in the nineteenth century. Standardization of construction is evident in the repetitive elements of a Chicago and North Western car of the late 1880s (below)

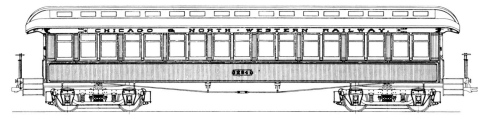

similar. It was not until the second half of the century that improvements were introduced, and the source of most of the innovations was the United States.

The American railway carriage, familiar from countless Western films, developed on a completely different pattern from the European, a typical example being a design for the Baltimore and Ohio Railroad of 1865. The most notable difference was that it was not compartmented. Access was from doors at either end, and a continuous central aisle ran along its length with double seats ranked on either side. The seats had reversible backs to allow for flexible grouping or rearrangement according to the direction of travel. A stove at one end provided heating, and there was a small WC compartment. A high clerestory roof with small windows gave extra light and headroom, and in this space, oil-lamps provided lighting at night. At each end of the carriage an open platform enabled passengers to enter and leave, and provided communication between carriages.

The Midland Railway four-wheel composite coach of 1874, by comparison, lacked the facilities of the American type and was still in the coachbuilding tradition, its compartmental construction, with many doors and different-sized windows, providing obstacles to rapid assembly. The Baltimore and Ohio coach was much more regular in appearance. Its windows were of a common pattern, as was the seating, both, like the open

17
18

19

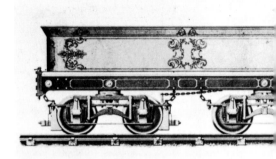

20 A typical American 4–4–0 locomotive of 1874 by the Baldwin company. Aesthetic emphasis was by applied decoration rather than formal composition of the structural elements, but the distinctive form and colourful grandeur of such designs made them a romantic symbol of the opening-up of the United States

plan with access limited to two points, making for ease of construction. All was plainly designed for industrial construction, combining large quantities of a limited number of standardized parts, in comparison with the handicraft methods of the British workshops.

Contributory reasons for the more open plan of American carriages, and the provision of basic services, were the longer duration of American journeys, and the climatic extremes between regions and seasons, necessitating greater attention to passenger comfort. In addition, traditional methods of construction were less influential in America than in Britain, since American coachbuilding was not completely supplanted on the advent of the railways. The country was so large that stage-coaches continued in use to provide widespread services, often acting as feeders to railway lines.

Comparisons of locomotive design practice in the United States and Britain are equally revealing. The 4–4–0 locomotive built by the Baldwin company from 1874 was representative of a type and form produced in large numbers in the United States in the late nineteenth century, and can be compared with the Johnson 4–4–0 for the Midland Railway. The function of the two engines is the same, but their form is very dissimilar. The openness of

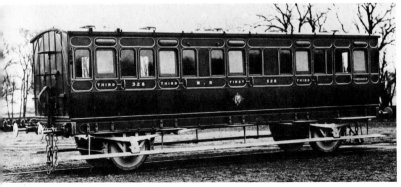

19 Midland Railway four-wheel composite coach of 1874 had advanced but little, except in size and third-class comfort

the Baldwin engine layout is a marked feature, giving clear access for maintenance, a vital necessity when running repairs might be required at points far from any workshop. The title of the man on the footplate in America reflected the need to repair the locomotive: he became known as an 'engineer'. In Britain he remained simply a 'driver', most of the routes he travelled never being more than a few miles from specialized repair facilities. The large, enclosed American cab was necessary for long-distance work under harsh climatic conditions, though a distinct aesthetic choice regarding its form was evident. Most American cabs of the period showed a preference for Renaissance forms, though one locomotive type experimented with Gothic Revival and pointed-arch windows. The so-called 'cow catcher' at the front of American locomotives was another characteristic feature. It hardly sufficed to deflect a large object on the line, but it could serve as a buffer, preventing obstacles from going under the wheels and derailing the train. The lamp at the front of the boiler was usually oil-burning and inefficient, casting a beam little more than a hundred yards, far less than a train's emergency stopping distance. Like the mandatory bell, however, it was a useful device in registering the approach of a train to man or beast, necessary because American lines went across open country, whereas British lines were fenced, protected by physical barriers and the laws of trespass. The inverted-cone shape of the American chimney was also markedly different from the British cylindrical form. American locomotives, particularly in the far West, generally used wood for fuel, being far from sources of coal. Wood, when burnt, produced more sparks than coal, a considerable fire risk in dry country, and a spark-arrestor fitted to the chimney gave it its distinctive shape.

What emerges from the comparison is that, in this instance, generalized equations between designed form and mechanical function cannot be sustained. In the two examples considered, a relationship certainly exists, but needs to be qualified and extended by examination of function in the particular physical, economic and cultural context. Neither can this relationship be considered as rigidly deterministic; there remains a considerable leeway for variations and aesthetic choice.

Shipping was also transformed in the nineteenth century, from timber sailing vessels to vast iron and steel structures powered by steam engines and turbines. Although naval architecture is not strictly an aspect of industrial design, ships were so frequently cited as examples of functionalist development that they deserve consideration.

In the earlier part of the century, sailing ships were often seen as symbols of harmony between man and Nature. Horatio Greenough, an American sculptor, wrote in an essay, *Form and Function*, in 1851: 'in art, as in nature, the soul, the purpose of a work will never fail to be proclaimed in that work in proportion to the subordination of the parts to the whole, of the whole to the function'. Beauty in ships: 'has been effected, first, by strict adaptation of forms to functions, second, by the gradual elimination of all that is irrelevant and impertinent'. In another essay, writing of clipper ships, he proclaimed: 'What Academy of Design, what research of connoisseurship, what imitation of the Greeks produced this marvel of construction? Here is the study of man upon the great deep, where Nature spake of the laws of building . . . and he bent all his mind to hear and obey.'

Beauty was equated with functionalism defined by Nature, in a Romantic, pantheistic sense. The clipper ships were certainly among the most beautiful creations of their age, but Greenough tended to ignore the degree of scientific calculation that went to determining their form, and the particular functional objectives for which they were designed. They were built for the opium trade with China, in which speed was necessary to evade government patrols and pirates alike; later they were used to transport tea from China and wool from Australia, trades where the earliest goods to reach their markets received the highest prices. Calculations concerned with speed thus dictated the form of the hull, overriding optimum requirements for the inner working-structure and organization of the ship, and in this secondary area, function had to be adapted to form.

North Atlantic liners were later cited as examples of functionalism by such disparate figures as Henry van de Velde and Le Corbusier. The latter included photographs of liners in his book *Towards a New Architecture* of 1923, with enthusiastic captions, such as 'An architecture pure, neat, clear, clean and healthy.' The great age of the liner began in the 1890s, and to many

21–2 The Hamburg-Amerika liner *Imperator* of 1913 was, at 52,000 tons, then the largest ship in the world. The imposing exterior structure was composed of a series of geometric volumes, in contrast to the florid decoration of the interior accommodation, designed to create the impression of a large sea-going hotel

architects and designers, these ships were the epitome of the modern age: sleek, functional and beautiful. The Hamburg-Amerika *Imperator* of 1913 was the culmination of a series of German vessels built to challenge the supremacy of the British Cunard line. However, the element of commercial and national rivalry led to the development of many features which cannot solely be explained in terms of utility. The imposing superstructure built amidships, and the size and number of funnels, were deliberately designed to create a powerful impression of grandeur.

A similar disparity is evident in the interior forms of liners. Their design related not only to essential considerations of seaworthiness and performance, but to the transport of passengers in surroundings providing comfort and reassurance. In fact, only the third-class and crew accommodation satisfied criteria of functional simplicity, the general standard being settings of sumptuous and even exotic richness, creating in essence a world of fantasy, with features such as smoking-rooms in the half-timbered style of Bavarian hunting-lodges or Tudor baronial halls, depending on nationality. Yet there was a logic to it all: no amount of comfort could relieve sea-sickness, or diminish the dangers of sea-voyaging, but it could reassure and divert. That, too, was an important function.

In railways and shipping, the relationship between form as mechanism or structure, and as decoration and symbol, is complex, interacting at a number of levels, and capable of being interpreted on the basis of different values. The popular form of transport at the end of the nineteenth century, the bicycle, was, however, simpler in both structure and function. This simplicity was the outcome of a concentrated period of experiment and development, taking place in several countries. Much early work concentrated on velocipedes, under various titles, of three wheels or more, driven by diverse and often fantastic looking means. Two-wheeled pedal-driven bicycles appeared first in France, and in the 1860s the 'ordinary', popularly known as the 'penny-farthing', enjoyed a widespread vogue. Its proportions, with a large wheel in front and small trailing wheel, were dictated by the pedal drive being directly connected to the front hub; the large front wheel was necessary to convert the thrust on the pedals into a speed adequate to enable the cyclist to maintain balance. Form was certainly related to mechanical function, but the latter was not very efficient. That and the precariously high seat limited its application.

After another wave of experiment in the 1870s, John Kemp Starley of Coventry produced the first modern bicycle, the 'safety', which successfully combined a series of separate innovations into a coherent whole. The main features were a diamond frame which gave great strength and rigidity, chain drive to the rear wheel, and direct steering through forward curving front

23 John Kemp Starley's Rover 'safety' bicycle of 1888 established a basic format for cycle design that is still used world-wide

wheel forks. It rapidly established itself with the public, and later innovations such as caliper brakes, variable gearing and air-cushioned tyres improved it further, making it the first individual form of mass-transportation.

The success of the 'safety' bicycle required an optimum combination of mechanical efficiency, lightness and durability, and these requirements had to be compatible with ease of manufacture. The introduction of mass-produced seamless tubular steel in the 1880s was a major factor in enabling a strong lightweight frame to be produced; but the simplicity of the form was above all due to the fact that, unlike the other examples discussed in this chapter, the bicycle was designed to fulfil a single function. This monofunctional character made it one of the apposite examples of the equation of form and function, the efficient performance of the bicycle's function affording very few opportunities for decoration.

The impact of technological innovation was also widely manifested in goods produced for domestic use, and it is here that the functionalist interpretation of form becomes more doubtful. The proposition that the products of mechanized manufacturing processes ought to be simple and functional in appearance was certainly not generally accepted in the nineteenth century. Some of the new industrial processes not only enabled a greater degree of decoration to be produced, but actually required decorative forms in order to overcome problems of processing, or in the materials used.

Furniture design illustrates aspects of this complexity. The early stages of quantity production involved adapting traditional forms and techniques and concentrating on producing a limited range within an enlarged commercial structure. The traditional 'Windsor chair' form in Britain and the United States, for example, was widely adapted to quantity production. It was made up of separate parts, most of which could easily be turned on a simple wood lathe, and the elemental simplicity of the form made it admirably adaptable to the available materials and technology. The difficulty in making the chair arose at the point of assembly, when the drilling of sockets and fitting together of parts required a high degree of skill. Lambert Hitchcock at Berkhamstead, Connecticut, developed a high rate of production by buying in the structural elements from sub-contractors and concentrating his resources on the skills of assembly. His factory, even in its early days, produced chairs at a rate of over fifty per day, at a cost of $1.50 apiece, and it is estimated that during Hitchcock's lifetime over a million were manufactured.

24, 25 One of the most famous examples of nineteenth-century design, the bentwood furniture produced by Michael Thonet's factories, was, in contrast, the result of the introduction of new technology. Thonet, born in the German Rhineland, began experiments in bending wood around 1830. Some of his early chairs were seen by the Austrian Prince Clemens Metternich at an exhibition at Koblenz in 1841. As a result, Thonet was

24–5 The structural simplicity of Michael Thonet's chair No. 14 of 1859, and its grace and proportion, made it one of the most popular designs ever produced (far left). Bentwood was capable of use for decorative effect, however, as in the sinuous lines of Thonet's chair No. 22 of the early 1870s (left)

invited to Vienna, where he patented his methods and in 1853 opened his own firm. Thonet's technique was indeed revolutionary: machine-formed rods of wood, usually beech, were curved and bent under steam-pressure and screwed together, completely eliminating the need for jointing or sockets. The simplicity of both the process and the forms produced enabled chairs to be manufactured in huge quantities, at low prices, and Thonet soon had a world market. His models were widely copied, and many remain in production by the same methods to the present day. The elegance and quality of Thonet's designs are indisputable, but they were in no way as 'inevitable' as they are often depicted, many models being highly decorative. *25* Neither was his production totally an expression of modern technology. In 1900, the firm employed four thousand workers who produced some six thousand items a day, a proportional relationship that reflects the extent of handwork still necessary in assembling frames and weaving the cane seats and backs of many of the classic models.

By 1900, over fifty firms in Austria were producing bentwood furniture. Less well known than Thonet, but a major competitor, was the Moravian firm of Jakob and Josef Kohn, founded in 1867, which specialized in bentwood furniture decorated by means of milling, engraving and sculptural techniques, and advertised as 'superior furniture in various styles'. Thus even homely bentwood could be adapted to the decorative taste of the age.

The adaptation of new processes to prevailing taste can also be observed in the furniture produced in the 1850s by John Henry Belter, another German *26* emigrant, who settled in New York and patented methods of forming papier

26 A chair in neo-rococo style by John Henry Belter of New York. Machine-pressed laminates were used to produce forms of great strength, curving in several directions, that were then hand-carved

mâché and laminated wood into complex shapes using steam-presses. These pieces were then hand-carved in intricate, open-work floral patterns in the then-fashionable neo-rococo taste. The perforated design that resulted was only made possible by the structural strength of the industrially produced materials and form, but was in no way a direct expression of them.

In other industries, new processes and techniques enabled a prodigious variety of designs to be manufactured, the products of some companies ranging from stark utilitarian forms to the most flamboyantly ornate. For example, in the pottery industry the moulding techniques evolved in North Staffordshire in the eighteenth century were further developed and applied to a great diversity of new forms. Henry Doulton's Lambeth Studio has already been mentioned, but its artistic achievement was, in fact, subsequent to the firm's rapid growth and the establishment of its reputation on the basis of producing wares for more utilitarian purposes. The squalor and disease of rapidly growing cities had required urgent measures, and in 1845 Doulton was persuaded to begin large-scale production of stoneware pipes for sewers and water conduits. It was a highly successful venture, followed by the production of a large range of domestic sanitary ware, and these two areas of production firmly established Doulton as a major manufacturer. The range and variety of designs for these products were enormous, catering for large institutions such as barracks and prisons as well as for domestic use across the social scale. Sinks, baths and lavatory pedestals were produced in a series of mouldings, some ornate, some simply utilitarian, though, as a page from 27 Doulton's 1898 catalogue shows, these latter could be colour-glazed or decorated with printed transfers to suit various tastes at marginally extra cost.

A similar commercial and design eclecticism prevailed in the glass industries that grew in size and production in the same period. The impact of technical innovation was less marked here until the industry began to be transformed radically in the last decades of the nineteenth century. Traditional blowing, cutting and engraving still placed a premium on a high level of craft skill. There were two innovations, however, that increased production and enlarged the range of forms. One was the technique of blowing into moulds, enabling bottles and containers to be produced repetitively at low cost to keep pace with the growing industrialization of brewing, food and medicament processing, and the increase in wine sales and home preserving. The second was the technique of pressing glass. Molten glass was placed in a heated brass or iron mould, and was formed by pressing a plunger into the mould. First developed in the United States in the mid-1820s, the method rapidly spread all over Europe. The technique could only be used for open shapes, such as glasses, bowls and trays, and a considerable

44

DOULTON'S
IMPROVED PEDESTAL "SIMPLICITAS WASH-DOWN"
CLOSET AND TRAP IN ONE PIECE.

No. 144.

No. 144A.

N.B.—In connecting Tank
to Closet 1¼ inch Pipe
must be used.

No. 144B.

No. 144J.

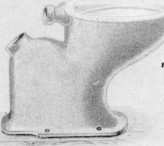

For Section showing
Distance of Outlet
from Wall,
see page 19.

Can be supplied with Turn-down (S) Trap as shown, or Shoot-out (P) Trap.

PRICES.

DOULTON'S IMPROVED "SIMPLICITAS" WASH-DOWN CLOSET AND TRAP, Complete.

In One Piece of Extra Strong Glazed Ware, with Flushing Rim

No. 144. —In plain Stoneware, White inside, Brown outside, with Pine Seat, No. 162 2-gallon
    Paisley Cistern, painted Brackets, and No. 53 Chain Pull, - - - each, £3 2 0
No. 144A.—Ditto, ditto, but with Blue Ornamentation, - - - - - - " 3 8 0
No. 144B.—Ditto Extra Strong Glazed Ware, White inside and Light Brown outside, - - " 3 8 6
No. 144C.—Ditto, ditto, ditto, White inside and outside, - - - " 3 15 0
No. 144J.—Ditto, ditto, ditto, ditto and Light Brown outside, with printed
    Ornamentation, - - - - - - - - - - - " 3 10 0

N.B.—In all cases Turn-down (S) Traps are sent with Closets unless otherwise ordered.
The above can be supplied with better Seats and Pulls if desired, see pages 32 and 35.

PRICES of BASIN and TRAP only.

No. 144. —Plain Stoneware, White inside and Brown outside, - - - - - each, £1 5 0
No. 144A.—Ditto, but with Blue Ornamentation, - - - - - - - " 1 11 0
No. 144B.—Extra Strong Glazed Ware, White inside and Light Brown outside, - - - " 1 11 6
No. 144C.—Ditto, ditto, White inside and outside, - - - - " 1 18 0
No. 144J.—Ditto, ditto, . ditto and Light Brown outside, with printed
    Ornamentation, - - - - - - - - - - - " 1 13 0

N.B.—If Basins and Traps only are required, this must be clearly specified, or Closets will be sent complete.
For Designs of Tiling, see pages 4, 6, 38, 57, 58, 59, 60, 61, 157, 158.

27 A page from Doulton's 1898 catalogue, illustrating the 'Simplicitas' range of water closets. The form of each model was produced from the same mould, differentiated by means of variegated finishes and decoration

initial problem was caused by the surface produced which was rough and matt. To offset this, a technique of decoration was developed in America that used raised dots and stippling, which evolved into a style known as 'lacy' glass. Production of pressed glass resulted in a rapid expansion of the industry in America; in 1820 there were twenty glass houses: by 1837 this number had increased to over one hundred. The overall result was a massive expansion of cheap glassware for everyday use. The pattern-designs of 'lacy' glass were not simply, as has been asserted, the manifestation of a nineteenth-century *horror vacuii*, but an appropriate and often handsome expression of materials and process. The forms and designs became multifarious as the exploitation of the technique and the development of high standards of workmanship led to greater assurance. A catalogue of the New England Glass Company of Boston, Massachusetts, published in 1869, displayed nearly fourteen hundred items, a page of the 'Union' pattern series illustrating the diversity of forms within a single range produced by this company.

28

Some glass companies manufactured both craft products and pressed glass, but the element of diversification is observable as a general feature, catering for a broad spectrum of needs and tastes, rather than concentrating on a limited range of forms. The English firm of Thomas Webb of Stourbridge included in their main series of patterns, between 1837 and 1900, over twenty-five thousand items of all kinds. At the Vienna World Exhibition of 1873, the internationally famous Austrian firm of J. & L. Lobmeyr exhibited fifty sets of drinking vessels, several dessert services and numerous other items in a variety of styles, ranging from the utmost simplicity to intricate patterns, and produced by several techniques. Most were designed by Ludwig Lobmeyr, the head of the firm, though he also commissioned leading artists, such as Theophil Hansen. The work of the firm was later to cover the spectrum from quantity production of plain everyday wares to the complete glass fittings, crystal chandeliers, wall lights and candelabra for two of 'Mad King' Ludwig II's castles, at Linderhof and Herrenchiemsee in Bavaria.

Above all else, innovation in metal technology facilitated a significant extension of formal possibilities and their application. Cast and wrought iron, and later steel, were the basic constituent materials, but the application and discovery of a growing range of other metals and alloys provided a continuously expanding repertoire of qualities and structural characteristics. The ductility of cast iron or the malleability of sheet steel, tin or brass made almost any form possible, and in metal design it becomes most abundantly clear that nineteenth-century concepts of form were not predominantly conditioned by the expressive possibilities of materials, or by production techniques, but, more than anything else, by notions of differentiated social

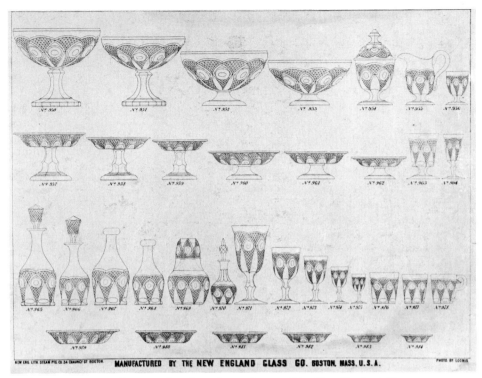

MANUFACTURED BY THE NEW ENGLAND GLASS CO. BOSTON, MASS. U.S.A.

28 Plate No. 18, one of twenty-five, from the catalogue of the New England Glass Company of Boston, 1869. The pattern used for the 'Union' range is known as 'bulls-eye and diamond point' and is found in many variants in pressed glass

function. This can be illustrated by comparing objects that have a similar nature, produced for different contexts. An oil-lamp, for example, used as a miners' safety lamp, or to clip on to a locomotive to indicate the nature of the train being hauled, would be of the utmost utilitarian simplicity consonant with its working task. A Colza oil-lamp produced in 1850 for domestic use, however, was decoratively moulded in such a way that the ingenious clockwork mechanism that automatically pumped oil to the wick was completely hidden. The catalogues of nineteenth-century cutlery manufacturers contained knives for kitchen use that were plain and unadorned, while those for use at table were in a variety of ornamental patterns. A similar contrast appeared between cast-iron stoves for heating kitchens and those for living-rooms – the list of examples is infinite. Although there are inevitably exceptions, utilitarian efficiency was generally the touchstone for working implements and artefacts, but in other aspects of

29–30 Social context rather than mechanical function is frequently a determinant of form. The simplicity of an oil-lamp used on Dutch railway locomotives in the late nineteenth century (left) is a marked contrast to the decorated lamp used to light the interiors of American passenger cars (above)

life, for leisure, relaxation and social intercourse, the ideal was a setting of art and refinement. This has sometimes subsequently been equated with class divisions on the basis that simplicity stems from working needs, does not differentiate, is available to all and therefore democratic; decoration is pretentious, associated with middle-class ostentation, and socially divisive. It is frequently true that the products of firms ranged in form from simplicity to decoration in order of ascending price, and therefore social accessibility; but even in British working-class homes, the furnishings and fittings of the parlour, a room set aside for rest days, celebrations or solemn occasions, followed the decorative taste of the age. A writer in a journal for artisans and mechanics asserted in 1840: 'Despite the Utilitarians, and their fine spun theories, and subtle arguments, we delight in painting and the kindred arts. Man was not created to spend his whole existence in toil.' A plain, functional form generally signified the often harsh necessities of work, and as such was tolerated in its place, but art, in the form of decoration and ornament, *29, 30* represented for many people a deep aspiration for a better life. The predominant aesthetic ideal of the nineteenth century in fact embodied a vision of harmony between utility and beauty that was articulated at length by Matthew Digby Wyatt in his book *Metalwork* of 1852, attacking with equal vigour what he defined as two classes of bigots, the Utilitarians who produced useful ugliness, and the Idealists who 'sacrifice comfort and convenience to ornament and effect'. Similar sentiments were echoed in more popular form by John Holland, a Sheffield poet, to whom the last word on this subject can be left. After visiting the Crystal Palace in 1851, he wrote a twenty-page account entitled, 'The Great Exhibition: A Poetical Rhapsody'. His verse was excruciating, but in a passage referring to the products of his native city he declaimed this general ideal of harmony:

> And since, in these utilitarian days,
> Men value most, what most they deem of use,
> Well may these keen edged wares claim equal praise,
> From the shrewd factor and the local muse:
> Utility! here dost thou hourly rove
> With beauty hand–in–hand by many a burnished stove.

CHAPTER THREE

The 'American system' and mass-production

As we have seen, the European response to industrialization was conditioned by a continuity of social and economic structures and attitudes. Craft techniques and processes were widely adapted and developed to produce large quantities of goods that, in form and design, reflected a conscious, if sometimes confused, recognition of past traditions. The significant and fundamental changes were mainly in the scale of commercial organization and production, rather than in the manufacturing methods by which goods were produced.

By the middle of the nineteenth century, however, largely as a result of the Great Exhibition of 1851, the rest of the world became aware of new methods of manufacture in the United States that established the fundamental patterns and processes of modern industrial mass-production. These were characterized by large-scale manufacture of standardized products, with interchangeable parts, using powered machine-tools in a sequence of simplified mechanical operations. The implications of this approach, which became widely known as the 'American system' of manufacture, were not confined to production methods, but also affected the whole organization and co-ordination of production, the nature of the work-process, the methods by which goods were marketed, and, not least, the type and form of the goods produced.

As with many developments in the United States, there were European precursors and influences. Around 1729, in Sweden, Christopher Pohlem had applied water-power to simple machine processes and precision measurement to produce interchangeable gears for clocks, at a factory in Stjärnsund. Later in the eighteenth century, a French armourer, known only as Le Blanc, applied similar methods to the production of muskets. After visiting Le Blanc's workshops in 1782, Thòmas Jefferson, then American Minister to France, noted in a letter: 'An improvement is here made in construction of muskets. . . . It consists in making every part of them so exactly alike, that what belongs to any one, may be used for every other musket in the magazine. . . . The advantages of this when arms need repair are evident.' Le Blanc's work met with considerable obstruction, however, from the official bureaucracy that administered government arsenals, and from craftsmen who saw their livelihood threatened.

French ideas were linked to English developments by one Marc Brunel, a Royalist refugee from the French Revolution, who designed machinery for the mass-production of pulley blocks for the Royal Navy, for Sir Samuel Bentham, then Inspector General of Naval Works and himself a pioneer inventor of many types of woodworking machinery. Once the exigencies of the Napoleonic Wars were past, however, the system was abandoned.

The basic approach was taken up in the United States around 1800, and was developed on a scale that thoroughly justifies its being called the 'American system'. Eli Whitney is often cited as its founder, largely on the basis of a proposal he made to the American government in 1798 for the manufacture of ten thousand muskets in two years (though in fact the contract was not completed until eleven years later). Research on surviving Whitney muskets indicates that the number of interchangeable parts was limited, and their precision, and thus the extent to which they were interchangeable, was variable. Other armourers in the United States, such as Simeon North and John Hancock Hall, were at least as advanced in their thinking, and probably more advanced in production methods. The truth would seem to be that, rather than any one person possessing a unique claim to having invented the system, it was an idea that had general currency at the time, emerging in a continuous series of improvements, each being eagerly seized on by competitors.

Hall, in particular, emphasized and developed the decisive elements permitting interchangeability, namely, precision measurement and accuracy in production. This work culminated in a simplified breechloading flintlock *31* introduced in 1824 and produced for twenty years. His stated intention was to 'make every similar part of every gun so much alike that it will suit every gun, so that if a thousand guns were taken apart and the links thrown together promiscuously on a heap, they may be taken promiscuously from the heap and will come right'. In order to do this, Hall had to simplify each part as far as possible, and his products are a marked utilitarian contrast to the elegant, decorated products of master gunsmiths. His methods were later

31 Flintlock rifle by John Hancock Hall, 1824. A precursor of mass-production

refined by firms that were to have international reputations in arms production, such as Sharp, Henry, Winchester and Remington.

The American system reached a high point of development by the mid-nineteenth century in another area of arms production – revolvers – with the establishment of Samuel Colt's armoury at Hartford, Connecticut. Colt was typical·of this generation of American innovators, taking principles and inventions that were widely available, and combining them with a form that was distinctive and totally effective. Other contemporary armourers produced excellent weapons, but it was Colt's thoroughgoing application of mass-production methods, and an exceptional flair for salesmanship and promotion, that made him so successful. His factory contained over fourteen hundred machine-tools, and under the leadership of Elisha K. Root, a technical genius, was a magnet for anyone interested in the most advanced methods of manufacture. The United States Secretary for War referred to it as having 'the status of a national work'. Colt's Navy .36 Revolver of 1851 is typical of his products. Like Hall's flintlock, it was reduced to an essential simplicity, and the precision of its interchangeable parts defined standards for the form of hand-weapons for many years.

The fact that the American system developed in relation to the production of firearms is, in retrospect, hardly surprising. The supply of large quantities of reliable and inexpensive weapons was a corollary of the general expansion of the size of military forces, and the constant series of wars against neighbouring states and native inhabitants of the West in which the United States was involved. The only significant application of the American system abroad was also in armaments, the British government establishing the Enfield manufactory with American machine-tools in 1853, and American equipment also being supplied to Prussia and France. Government contracts were necessary in order to pay for the plant and equipment initially required to set up the new system.

What was unique to the United States, however, was the adaptation of the system to other areas of manufacture unsupported by government funds. In

32 Colt's Navy .36 revolver of 1851. Although it is hand-engraved as a presentation piece the basic simplicity is still evident

33 Chauncey Jerome eight-day clock
with cherry-wood case of the late 1840s

part, this was due to a lack of skilled labour and the absence of an entrenched craft tradition. Samuel Colt, in discussions with British engineers, stated that uneducated workers were best suited to the new mass-production methods since they had so little to unlearn. Innovation was not a challenge to established institutions and habits in the young Republic, and in an open, expanding society the commercial opportunities for wealth and advancement were a strong inducement. A British commission investigating the American system in 1853 noted 'the dissatisfaction frequently expressed in America with regard to present attainment in the manufacture and application of labour-saving machinery, and the avidity with which any new idea is laid hold of, and improved upon . . .'.

By 1850 the American system had spread to other industries in New England, the centre of arms production, and later appeared in other districts. It was introduced to the manufacture of clocks in the 1830s by Eli Terry, who produced a clock movement from wooden parts, and in the following decade Chauncey Jerome took the process a step further by introducing *33* metal gears stamped from thin, rolled-brass sheet, instead of brass castings. This resulted in a less bulky movement, and the clocks produced were very slim, suitable for wall-hanging without undue protuberance. The cases of plain wood were also mass-produced.

By 1838 the first attempt had been made to mass-produce watches, though with little success, the finer movements presenting greater difficulties. It was not until 1850 that sustained production began, started by the American Horologe Company of Roxbury, Massachusetts. Aaron L. Dennison, one of its founders, had visited the Springfield Armoury and decided that watches, as well as guns, could be made by mass-production methods. His pocket-watches with movement plates die-punched from rolled brass by steam-powered machinery had circular metal frames that

34 A section of the American stand at the Great Exhibition, 1851, showing Goodyear's and Colt's highly successful exhibits

could be hand-engraved for more expensive models, and printed metal dials with numerals in various typographic styles. By the end of the century the manufacture of watches was a major industry, the Waterbury company producing half a million a year, and the Ingersoll company marketing a watch that cost only one dollar. They were accessible to the whole population.

Some of the most dramatic effects resulted from the mass-production of agricultural machinery, an area that the Americans constantly improved and refined. In 1819 Jethro Wood of Scipio, New York, patented a cast-iron plough built from separated standardized and interchangeable parts. The most spectacular developments, however, radically influenced grain production. In 1833–4 both Obed Hussey and Cyrus McCormick produced practical reaping machines. By the 1850s these machines were mass-produced and being sold as fast as they could be manufactured. McCormick's was the most successful, selling about four thousand a year, a high figure for a relatively complicated mechanism.

American products were often criticized by European observers for their lack of finish and solidarity, their use of substitute materials, and their cheapness. The Great Exhibition of 1851 in London, however, marked a turning-point in attitudes. The exhibits for the American stand were assembled hastily and late, and were inadequate to fill the large space booked, causing considerable derision in the London press. The opportunity to study the products on show over a long period of time, however, enabled them to be taken more seriously, and by the end of the exhibition some had earned considerable respect, in particular Goodyear's rubber products, Colt's revolvers and the McCormick reaper. The rest of the world began to sit up and take notice, and the British Commission that subsequently visited the United States was to warn: 'the Americans display an amount of ingenuity,

combined with undaunted energy, which as a nation we would do well to imitate, if we mean to hold our present position in the great market of the world'.

The difference between Europe and America was not limited, however, to production systems, but applied in a much wider sense to general cultural and social values. This was remarked on in the Official Catalogue of the Great Exhibition: 'The expenditure of months or years of labour upon a single article, not to increase its intrinsic value, but solely to augment its cost or its estimation as an object of *virtu*, is not common in the United States. On the contrary, both manual and mechanical labour are applied with direct reference to increasing the number or the quantity of articles suited to the wants of a whole people, and adapted to promote the enjoyment of that moderate competency which prevails upon them.' The comparison was between European attitudes, based on craft traditions, in which the value of a product, both economically and aesthetically, resided in the extent of skilled work it embodied, and the American approach, based on industrial methods, which emphasized quantity and utility for wider sections of the population. But was it true to say, as the catalogue asserted, that this difference gave 'the productions of American industry a character distinct from that of other countries'? In the opinion of George Wallis, a member of the British Commission of 1853, and head of the Birmingham School of Art and Design, a clear distinction had to be drawn between the means of production, in which he recognized the unique American achievement, and the goods produced, which he regarded as a reflection of prevailing European taste. The types of manufacture upon which he concentrated, however, were all traditional areas of European decorative art – furniture, metalware, ceramics, glassware and jewellery – in which American producers had to compete with European imports. In such areas of production, technical and

35–6 I. M. Singer's first sewing machine of 1851 was crude but efficient. In contrast, the Singer 'New Family' of *c.* 1870 was transformed into a marketable product

commercial innovation did not inevitably lead to new forms. Wallis' judgment of the industries he considered was accurate and perceptive. At the time he made his report, however, the results of American ingenuity were beginning to be manifested in completely new products that did not fit comfortably into the European concept of decorative art, and these products were to proliferate to an extent that demanded attention. A crucial example was the sewing machine.

The process of sewing by hand requires a constant and subtle interplay of material, hand and eye. Many attempts had been made to replicate this manual dexterity by mechanical means, but it was not until 1844 when Elias Howe, a skilled mechanic from Boston, developed a needle with the eye placed at the point, using two to make an interlocking stitch below the surface of the material, that a mechanical sewing machine became feasible. After many vicissitudes, Howe finally managed to put his machine into production with considerable success. The idea was also taken up by Isaac Merrit Singer, who refined Howe's design, and by placing the sewing action on a vertical axis gave the machine its definitive form. Like Samuel Colt, Singer combined mechanical ingenuity with commercial flair. Realizing the potential of sewing machines, he marketed them with unflagging vigour, introducing what now seems an inevitable feature of modern life: hire purchase. The mass-production and sales generated by Singer also brought formal changes in his products. His first machine of 1851 was a very plain,

35

56

functional mechanism, but an appreciation of the importance of appearance led to the mechanism being shrouded in a pressed, japanned-metal casing, decorated with stencilled floral patterns. The stand and foot-treadle drive, produced as optional extras, also had patterns of scrolls and latticework, designed to make them more acceptable in a domestic setting. The basic form of Singer's machines was dictated by mechanical function, but presentation conformed to conceptions of what was aesthetically appropriate to the social context in which the machines were used. 36

An interesting contrast is presented by another contemporary machine that radically altered working patterns: the typewriter. Like the sewing machine, it was the result of a long process of invention and refinement. In 1873 a machine built by Sholes and Glidden, which resolved many outstanding problems, was demonstrated to Philo Remington, whose family firm was well established as manufacturers of weapons, sewing machines and agricultural machinery. With the post-Civil-War slump in arms production, Remington was seeking new products, and signed a contract to produce the typewriter. Two of his best mechanics, William K. Jenne and Jefferson M. Clough, were assigned to the task of redesigning the machine 37 for mass-production. They had been working on sewing machines, and the influence of that work is evident in the form and decoration of the casing, stand, and the treadle that operated the carriage change. The success of the typewriter was less immediate than that of the sewing machine, but eventually it came to be used extensively in the different visual context of business premises. As a result it evolved into a starker, non-decorated form, such as the Remington No. 10 of 1907, which reverted to a more 38 emphatically functional appearance.

37–8 Remington's first typewriter (left), derived from designs by C.L. Sholes and C. Glidden, appeared in 1874. Decorative features were eliminated in the Remington No. 10 of 1907 (right)

By 1870 the American system was well established in over twenty industries, including, in addition to the examples already cited, precision instruments and tools; machine-tools, especially woodworking machinery; railroad cars of the type discussed in the previous chapter; cutlery, using rollers to press out the form in a continuous process instead of stamping; musical instruments such as pianos and melodions, and domestic hardware. It was to spread even further as the pace of industrial growth in the United States increased at an explosive rate. The expansion of business stimulated the mass-production of simple, efficient office-furniture: desks, bureaux, filing cupboards, swivel chairs and adjustable typists' chairs. New inventions were avidly adopted. Some, such as bicycles, were produced by firms with existing and appropriate experience and equipment; others, such as telephones and phonographs, were to form the basis of new industries.

Photography, for example, was first popularized by George Eastman with his lightweight Kodak camera of 1888 incorporating a ready-loaded film. This feature had the disadvantage, however, of requiring the camera to be returned to the manufacturer for processing. A new method of loading, using roll-film, enabled a mass-produced camera, the Folding Pocket Kodak, to be produced in 1895. It was followed in 1900 by the Brownie, intended by its designer, Frank Brownell, to be suitable for children. The plain black box was an appropriate expression of the total simplicity and inexpensiveness of the apparatus, which de-mystified photography and made it accessible to the amateur.

39
40

Not all mass-produced goods were so utilitarian, however; many of them catered equally for the fashionable taste for ornamentation and decoration. This decorative tendency has often been criticized as a degeneration in taste, though dismissive judgments do little to provide an understanding of why it occurred in America.

In part it was due to the growth of the United States into a complex and diverse society, conscious of its standing in the world, and seeking a sense of cultural identity. An aesthetic eclecticism was capable of reflecting these diversities and aspirations, and if European examples were followed, it was hardly surprising. Disparaging comments by European visitors on the cultural deficiencies and alleged materialism of Americans did much to create a sense of inferiority, a feeling that 'culture' was something extraneous, and a desirable acquisition. Participation in international exhibitions with the inevitable comparisons these provoked, importation of goods, publications and pattern books, and the large numbers of European immigrants, were all influential factors. The European suspicion of machine products was also implanted in Americans through the writings of John Ruskin and William Morris. Simple and utilitarian products were regarded

39 Folding Pocket Kodak camera, 1895

40 Kodak Brownie camera, 1900

as evidence of the 'mere materialism' of which Americans were often accused. As in Europe, however, aesthetic symbols and allusion did not necessarily restrict efficiency. Frank Leslie in his *Historical Register of the Centennial Exposition of 1876* in Philadelphia, commended the 'application of art ideas' to gas implements and processes in the Mitchell Vance Company's exhibit. Much decoration remained just that, impairing neither the function of products nor the American enthusiasm for, and pursuit of, innovation.

The ability to combine efficiency and embellishment was clearly demonstrated in the furniture designs of firms clustered around the city of Grand Rapids, Michigan, which became the major centre of American furniture production in the late nineteenth century. The industry was based on a high degree of mechanization, with considerable technical and organizational ingenuity evident in the production process. In a study of its development Kenneth L. Ames has pointed out two special requirements in the design of Grand Rapids furniture, that were also characteristic of many other products: it had to appear familiar yet embody some unique feature, and have an appearance of quality without being expensive to make. Mechanization, he argued, was the key to satisfying these requirements. 'If an elaborate piece of furniture could be made primarily by machine, with a minimum of hand labor, it could be offered to the public at a modest price.' In the competitive mass-market for furniture created by Grand Rapids firms,

41 Chamber suite by the Phoenix Furniture Company, Grand Rapids, 1878. Plain rectangular forms reveal its origin in mass-production techniques

close attention to public taste was necessary, and design was correspondingly given great emphasis. Ames quotes a writer of 1887 on this subject: 'Each establishment maintains its own staff of designers and they are busy the whole year round planning articles of furniture as comfortable, unique and beautiful as the art of man can compass.' Typical of the eclectic use of *41* Renaissance forms that dominated fashion in the 1870s was a chamber suite by the Phoenix Furniture Company, made in walnut. The pieces were sturdy and solid, and the height of the headboard and mirror-stand created an impression of stateliness. Decorative effect was achieved by jig-saw cut outlines, with turned roundels and cut panels glued to the basic structure. Innumerable designs for furniture of all kinds were produced in variations of the style, and became exceedingly popular.

A unified aesthetic in relation to mass-production did not, therefore, exist; in fact, the American system of manufacture catered for and encouraged diversity and eclecticism by the new modes of commercial organization and

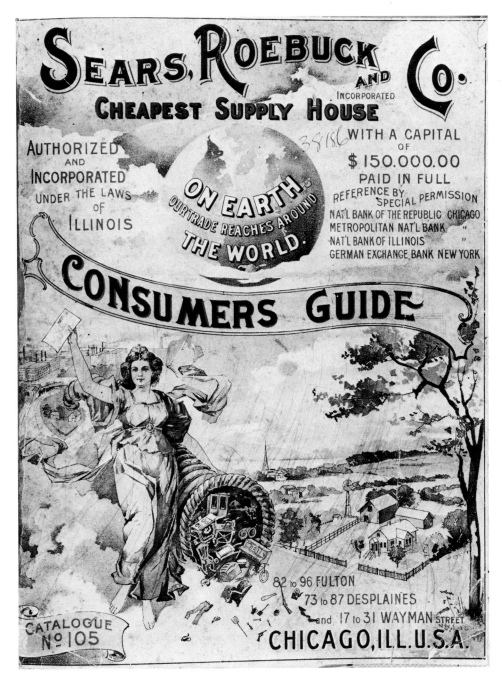

42 Cover of Sears, Roebuck Fall catalogue, 1897. The cornucopia was an apt image for the vast range of goods it made available to remote areas.

sales technique that it stimulated. Mass-production required mass-consumption, and there followed the establishment of department stores in cities, and later, mail order firms such as Montgomery Ward, founded in 42 1872, and Sears, Roebuck, founded in 1886. Both were established in Chicago at the hub of the railway system, and sold a vast range of products that catered for all a family's needs, across a wide geographical area.

With such highly competitive methods of selling, aesthetic appearance became a vital means of attracting interest. All tastes had to be catered for, and ever more complex and detailed effects became technically possible. The 43 Montgomery Ward catalogue of 1895 offered fifty-six different kinds of clocks, many by leading manufacturers such as Seth Thomas and the Waterbury company, ranging from simple alarm clocks to extravagantly decorated wall and mantel models, the casing finishes including oak, walnut, enamelled iron and gilt. Different exterior forms often housed the same movement, as with the 'Dakota' and 'Cato' models. Sears, Roebuck followed a similar policy. The 1906 catalogue section on sewing machines contained a paragraph under the heading 'Design' for each machine and cabinet, commenting on the 'Minnesota B' model that it was 'extremely handsome and pleasing in appearance, the general design being worked out in easy curves and rounded corners so as to avoid any suggestions of harshness or angularity'. The cabinet was described as a 'model of beauty and artistic design'.

Towards the end of the century, the full consciousness of the extent to which mechanization and the American system were effecting a transformation of the environment led to attempts to arrive at a machine-aesthetic. An important figure in formulating and disseminating this aesthetic was the architect Frank Lloyd Wright. He had worked under Louis Sullivan, whose famous dictum 'form follows function' was to become one of the great polemical slogans of modern architecture and design. Often misinterpreted as expressing a somewhat crude structural and aesthetic determinism, Sullivan's phrase, in the context of his argument, was an attempt to formulate a concept of organic unity in architecture in which function, structure and appropriate decoration could be fused to give an artistic expression appropriate to the modern age. Wright adopted and developed this organic concept, and his early independent work included designs for furniture and fittings intended to be an integral part of the houses he designed. These, like his buildings, were based on the massing of simple 44 elements. The chair built for his studio around 1895 by a Milwaukee cabinet-maker was an expression of Wright's interest at that time in the Arts and Crafts movement and in handicraft. He came to realize, however, that the clean, straight lines of his furniture could be better achieved by the precision

CLOCK DEPARTMENT—Continued.

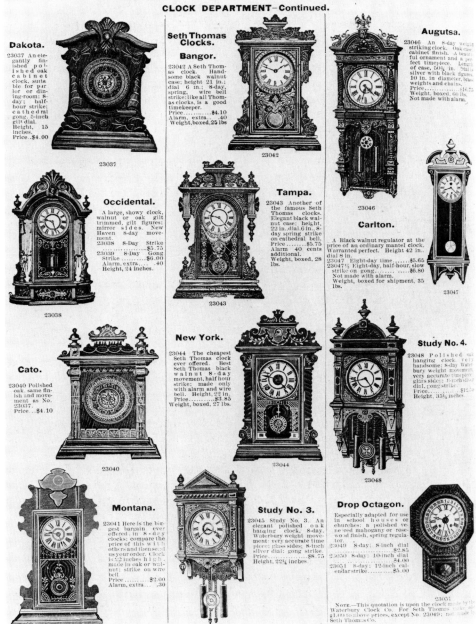

Dakota.

23037 An elegantly finished polished oak cabinet clock, suitable for parlor or dining-room; 8-day; half-hour strike; cathedral gong, 5-inch gilt dial. Height, 15 inches. Price..$4.00

Occidental.

A large, showy clock, walnut or oak gilt trimmed, gilt figures; mirror sides. New Haven 8-day movement.
23038 8-Day Strike
..............$5.75
23039 8-Day Gong Strike........$6.00
Alarm, extra... .40
Height, 24 inches.

Cato.

23040 Polished oak, same finish and movement as No. 23037.
Price...$4.10

Montana.

23041 Here is the biggest bargain ever offered in 8-day clocks; compare the price of this with others and then send us your order. Clock is 22 inches high, made in oak or walnut; strike on wire bell
Price........$2.00
Alarm, extra... .30

Seth Thomas Clocks.

Bangor.

23042 A Seth Thomas clock. Handsome black walnut case; height 21 in.; dial 6 in.; 8-day, spring, wire bell strike; like all Thomas clocks, is a good timekeeper.
Price.............$4.10
Alarm, extra..... .40
Weight, boxed, 25 lbs.

Tampa.

23043 Another of the famous Seth Thomas clocks. Elegant black walnut case; height 22 in., dial 6 in., 8-day spring strike on cathedral bell.
Price.......$5.75
Alarm 40 cents additional.
Weight, boxed, 28 lbs.

New York.

23044 The cheapest Seth Thomas clock ever offered. Best Seth Thomas black walnut 8-day movement, half hour strike; made only with alarm and wire bell. Height, 22 in.
Price...........$3.85
Weight, boxed, 27 lbs.

Study No. 3.

23045 Study No. 3. An elegant polished oak hanging clock, 8-day. Waterbury weight movement; very accurate time piece; glass sides; 8-inch silver dial; gong strike.
Price...............$8.75
Height, 22½ inches.

Augutsa.

23046 An 8-day weight striking clock. Oak cabinet finish. A beautiful ornament and a perfect timepiece. Length of case, 50½ in. Dial silver with black figures, 10 in. in diameter, brass weights and chains.
Price.............$16.75
Weight, boxed, 60 lbs.
Not made with alarm.

Carlton.

A Black walnut regulator at the price of an ordinary mantel clock. Warranted perfect. Height 42 in. dial 8 in.
23047 Eight-day time $5.65
23047½ Eight-day, half-hour, slow strike on gong........ $6.80
Not made with alarm.
Weight, boxed for shipment, 35 lbs.

Study No. 4.

23048 Polished oak hanging clock, very handsome; 8-day Waterbury weight movement; very accurate timepiece; glass sides; 8-inch silver dial, gong strike.
Price................$12.?0
Height, 35¼ inches.

Drop Octagon.

Especially adapted for use in school houses or churches; a polished veneered mahogany or rosewood finish, spring regulator.
23049 8-day; 8-inch dial
...................$2.85
23050 8-day; 10-inch dial
...................$4.00
23051 8-day; 12-inch calendar strike........$5.00

NOTE.—This quotation is upon the clock made by the Waterbury Clock Co. For Seth Thomas add $1.00 to above prices, except No. 23049; not made by Seth Thomas Co.

43 A page from Montgomery Ward's catalogue of 1895

of machines than by hand. In a famous lecture given in Chicago in 1901, 'The Art and Craft of the Machine', Wright expressed his positive attitude to mechanization and its potential for aesthetic expression, mounting a scathing attack on the misuse of machines to produce 'butchered forms' from past cultures. The machine, argued Wright, was 'the creature, not the Creator of this iniquity'. It was a tool whose potential effect was to emancipate the modern mind. Through its tendency to simplify, the machine could reveal the true nature and beauty of materials. Taking wood as an instance, 'machines have undoubtedly placed within reach of the designer a technique enabling him to realize the true nature of wood in his designs harmoniously with man's sense of beauty, satisfying his material needs with such economy as to put this beauty of wood in use within the reach of everyone'.

For Wright, there was no contradiction between individual values and mass-production. He argued that the provision of a better life for everyone and a diminution of human drudgery were essential for the flowering of a democratic culture. 'What limits do we dare imagine to an Art that is organic fruit of an adequate life for the individual?' But for this potential to be realized, it was necessary that artists grasp and utilize creatively the power of the machine. Wright's romantic view of the artist's role took little account, however, of the realities of the industrial context in which mechanization was applied; and his success in building up a practice dependent largely on private commissions meant that an opportunity never arose for him to attempt to realize his ideals in terms of industrial production.

44 Arm-chair designed by Frank Lloyd Wright, c. 1895. Although craft-made, its simple elegance indicates the emergence of his machine-aesthetic

Nevertheless his ideas, particularly those relating to mechanization, had wide currency in the United States and Europe, and anticipated many of the central tenets of the Modern Movement of the 1920s. There were, however, several contradictions in Wright's arguments, as in those of the Modern Movement. The assertion that simple, geometric forms were alone appropriate to machine production took little account of the wide potential of modern mechanical technology. Wright's inflexible application of his aesthetic principles to some of his later designs resulted in some exceedingly uncomfortable geometric furniture. More fundamentally, although he appreciated the potential benefits of the products of modern industry in contributing to better conditions of life, he failed to perceive the human cost that the new methods of production entailed. In 1812 Eli Whitney had clearly stated the objective of the American system of manufacture as, to 'substitute correct and effective operations of machinery for that skill of the artist which is acquired only by long practice and experience'. At the same time as Wright was formulating his arguments, the American system was reaching a culminating point in the fulfilment of that objective.

Throughout most of the nineteenth century the progress of the American system had emphasized the analysis of objects and mechanisms, breaking them down into interchangeable constituent parts and designing them for mechanized mass-production. Between 1880 and 1900 an engineer, Frederick W. Taylor, began a series of studies of work-processes in which he sought to find 'the one best way' of performing tasks; in other words, to achieve a standardization of working methods in order to maximize production. By timing the most efficient workers by stop-watch and seeking to eliminate superfluous movements, he was in fact seeking to integrate human capacities into the sequence of machine operations. This marked a complete rejection of the craft concept of work, which depends upon the skill, judgment and responsibility of individuals. Taylor's methods became widely known in the early years of the present century under the title 'scientific management', and were widely adopted. The adverse reaction they frequently aroused among workers, however, was to lead to an important modification, discussed in the following chapter, to take account of the harm to efficiency caused by fatigue depending not only on physical but also on psychological factors.

Co-ordination of all work-processes in pursuit of improved efficiency and production was first fully developed in the production of motor cars. The United States came late in the field of automobile manufacture, most of the initial development taking place in Europe, but it was in America that the low-priced mass-produced car emerged with astonishing rapidity. Early vehicles were individually craft-built in limited quantities. In 1901, however,

The OLDSMOBILE

Pioneer and Premier in Automobile construction and results. Starts at will, always under perfect control. Covers roughest roads without difficulty —just as useful in winter as in summer. Forty miles on one gallon of gasoline,—odorless, noiseless, strong. Carries fifteen hundred pounds easily and safely. **Price $650.**

Write for book. Address Dept. C.

OLDS MOTOR WORKS, Detroit, Mich.

THE OLDSMOBILE
Pioneer Gasoline Runabout
For Practical Business Use.

45 Ransome E. Olds' 'Oldsmobile' car as advertised in 1902

45 Ransome E. Olds began to produce a small, lightweight car on a mass-production basis in Detroit. The machine was very basic and designed for non-mechanically minded customers, with a curved dashboard and folding hood clearly derived from horse-drawn carriage forms, and tiller steering. Six hundred were sold in 1901, rising to 6,500 in 1905. It was a staggering achievement at the time, and opened up motoring to a broad public.

Olds' achievement was, however, to be dwarfed by Henry Ford's. The 'Oldsmobile' was only suitable for urban conditions and good roads; Ford

47 A section of the Ford production line assembling steering units, 1913

set out to design a car to cater specifically for a mass-market and the most rugged conditions. The outcome, in 1908, was the 'Model T'. From the first *46* it was tremendously popular, and Ford and his team set out to produce it as cheaply as possible. As a result, in 1914 they brought together the constituent parts of the modern mass-production system: quantity production of a *47* standard design with interchangeable parts, on a moving assembly line, to the pace and nature of which the workers were compelled to adapt.

The formula was decisive in increasing the volume of production and decreasing unit cost: in 1910 almost twenty thousand Model Ts were produced at a cost of $850 each; in 1916, nearly six hundred thousand at $360 each; before production ceased in 1927, nearly fifteen million had rolled off the production lines.

In design terms the Model T belonged to an interim stage: the influence of carriage design was still strong, for instance, in the spoked wheels and tonneau body with its folding hood; the body sat high on the chassis, in order to provide adequate clearance on poor rural roads; the bonnet was small, and the connecting panel to the body appeared ill-co-ordinated. But if the Model T was not the most beautiful car of its age, it was the most powerful symbol; the harbinger of a transformation in industrial work and industrial products that was to exceed anything previously experienced.

46 Henry Ford's 'Model T', 1908

CHAPTER FOUR

Standardization and rationalization

The evolution of the American system demonstrated that in order to be mass-produced, a product had to be standardized, i.e. designed to precise, invariable dimensions. With the growth in scale of industrial production and commercial organization in the twentieth century, the concept of standardization became extended, taking on new meanings and significance.

In the early stages of industrialization, each firm producing goods and machines established its own specification for the manufacture of parts and fittings, resulting in a plethora of dimensions and types of connections, and requiring users to maintain a huge stock of replacements to cover the different formats. A pioneering attempt to introduce order into the confusion was Sir Joseph Whitworth's system of standardized thread-measurements for nuts, bolts and screws, which was generally adopted in Britain and her territories with beneficial results. In the United States a different system, devised by William Sellars, was adopted in the 1870s, on the grounds that Whitworth's system required a high degree of craft skill in production to achieve the necessary accuracy, whereas Sellars' could be mass-produced accurately, cheaply and by unskilled labour using automatic machinery.

The adoption of these systems of technical standards was essential if the primary rationale of large-scale production, namely interchangeability, was to be effective on a national scale. This was to be made very clear to the Prussian government in the course of the war with France in 1870–1. The Prussian railway system had been established by a mixture of public and private enterprise, with nine state and numerous private companies, each with their own types of locomotives and rolling-stock. Mobilization and utilization for military purposes revealed the full incompatibility of the various stock, with concomitant problems of maintenance and repair under war conditions. Pressure from the military command led to the nationalization of the system and its formation into the Prussian State Railways. The new state system inherited the stocks of its component companies, all inadequate for the required programme of operation and extension. It therefore embarked on the development of a set of 'Prussian standards' which encompassed not only technical parts, but also the design and production of a series of standard types of locomotives and rolling stock for each category of use. The first standard locomotive appeared in 1877; and thereafter, not only was each succeeding type produced in large numbers, with considerable cost advantages in manufacture and operation, but, wherever possible, standardized components were utilized for several types, thus increasing interchangeability. If the approach to visual appearance was more utilitarian than in Britain, with a greater amount of exposed mechanism and controls, the proportions were generally well balanced and symmetrical, and the standardized elements introduced a degree of formal unity.

The advantages of standardization were subsequently to be appreciated by many large industrial and commercial concerns, most notably by the large electrical goods firms that emerged in the late nineteenth century, such as Siemens and the Allgemeine Elektrizitäts Gesellschaft (AEG). In the early years of the twentieth century both firms established an extensive range of standards for their internal operations, and in the case of AEG, the idea was exploited for products designed for domestic use.

48 In 1908 Cadillac gave a remarkable demonstration of standardization and interchangeability for the Royal Automobile Club of Britain. Three cars were dismantled and their components were mixed with spares. After reassembly the cars ran perfectly on a five-hundred-mile test

49–52 Peter Behrens' design for an AEG electric table-fan of 1908 (right) was a refinement of an existing form rather than an original conception, with cleaner lines and the gleam of brass fan-blades, guard and beading highlighted by the dark-green colour of the metal housing. With Behrens' electric kettles for AEG produced from 1909 (far right), the combination of standard elements pointed towards new methods of industrial design, while the hammered surface-effect and wound cane handles were stylistic devices based on craft forms and techniques

In 1907 Peter Behrens, a leading architect and designer, was appointed artistic adviser to AEG with a brief that gave him responsibility for the company's buildings, graphics and product-design. If the forms of the products he designed were not strongly innovatory – his electric fans and arc lamps, for instance, were dominated by their technical function and were basically similar to competitors' products – his sensitive handling of materials, colour and detail lent aesthetic distinction to technical form. With his electric kettles, however, we find something new. Once again there are marked similarities to competitors' external forms; there seems to have been tacit agreement on prevailing consumer taste. Behrens, however, designed his kettles on the basis of standardized elements that could be combined flexibly to give over eighty variations (although in fact only thirty were offered for sale). There were three kettle-forms, and two each of lids, handles and plinths. Three materials, brass, nickel-plate and copper-plate, were offered, each with three surface finishes, smooth, hammered and waved. There was a choice of three different sizes. The plugs and heating elements were common to all. It was the exploitation of the possibilities of combining a limited number of standard components to provide a broad product-range that made Behrens' work innovatory, and that distinguished him as one of the first industrial designers in the modern sense.

By the early twentieth century the concept of standardization was firmly established in a number of ways. Technical measurements, or basic standards, and specifications for connections to ensure interchangeability, tended to be established on a national level, by bodies set up to determine and

49

50–2

publicize such standards. In 1902 the British Engineering Standards Association, later to grow into the British Standards Institute, was founded. In 1916 the Deutsche Normen Ausschuss (German Standards Commission) began an extensive process of standardization on a national basis, the necessity of which was once again brought home by military pressure during the First World War. In the United States, the American Standards Association was founded in 1918, strongly supported by the Secretary of Commerce and later President, Herbert Hoover, himself an engineer by training. The constitution of these bodies, and the degree of government support and participation, varied, but generally they attempted to define standards by the agreement of all interested parties on the basis of the best of existing practice. The application of standards was usually voluntary, though in the Soviet Union from 1930 onwards, appreciation of their importance in the crash programme of industrialization under the Five Year Plans led to their definition by a state organization and enforcement by decree.

Standardized components or types, on the other hand, were pre-dominantly determined internally by large firms and were specific to the producers. In the United States, a struggle developed between large and small producers within the standards committee set up in 1905 by the Society of Automobile Engineers. Small producer-members who operated on the basis of assembling bought-in components did not want to be dependent upon one supplier, and therefore proposed a wide-ranging programme to standardize components, and even suggested standard designs for cars. The large concerns, however, were increasingly capable of producing their own components, and were chiefly interested in the standardization of basic norms and material quality. As the large firms expanded, swallowing up the small producers in the process, the pressure for intra-industry standardization slackened; but nevertheless a wide measure of agreement was achieved, and in the large corporations the process of defining internal standards was extended. The suggestion of standard designs, however, though put forward as a measure to protect the small producer, seemed to many people to be a logical outcome of the process of standardization, and they could point for support to the outstanding success of Henry Ford. Because his system of production depended upon the assembly line, with the automobile put together from a series of sub-units such as frame, engine, transmission and body, precise standardization was implicit. Ten years after the introduction of the Model T, Ford could argue that only by being exempt from commercial demand for a change of form could the car be built cheaply, utilizing special machine-tools of great cost.

Belief in the commercial necessity for standard design could be sustained as long as one firm had such an enormous lead in the market. Even in 1921, Ford still produced fifty per cent of all automobiles in the United States. His lead began to be eroded, however, as the industry consolidated into a small number of large producers, each organized on the basis of mass-production and all competing vigorously. Ford hung on obstinately to the Model T, but declining sales finally forced his hand. In 1927 came the 'Model A', followed in 1932 by the 'V8', which in turn was replaced by another V8 model in 1933. The diminishing interval between new models is indicative of the erosion of Ford's belief that changes of form were unnecessary.

53
54

The automobile industry seemed to be caught between two antithetical demands. On one hand, there was the demand for cheapness, requiring standardization, at least in the medium term, to absorb the massive investment in plant required for volume-production (though even so, such plant needed to be sufficiently flexible to take advantage of the rapid pace of technical innovation). On the other hand, the demand for novelty required rapid changes of model in order to sustain the interest of customers. It was from the unlikely parentage of these two pressures that 'styling' was born: the introduction of frequent changes of external style that emphasized aesthetic appearance, leading to the annual merry-go-round of 'new' models that yet allowed a measure of constancy in the production of technical components.

The effects of the second demand can be seen in three of the models produced by Ford within a decade. With the Model A of 1927 the heritage of its predecessor was still evident in the square, upright cab and the awkward

53 Ford 'Model A' car of 1927

54 Ford 'V8' car, 1933

55 Lincoln 'Zephyr', 1936. The Lincoln company was a subsidiary of Ford and run by Henry's son Edsel. His enthusiasm for styling found freer expression in Lincoln designs than in the main company still dominated by his father

linking-panel of the bonnet, though it was much more compact. The V8 of 1933 is appreciably changed, however, being larger, better integrated and having a greater air of assurance; the flow of the mudguards is emphasized and linked by the running-board, the reclining angle of bonnet and windscreen reflected in the lines of doors and radiator-louvres. The streamlined Lincoln Zephyr of 1936, in contrast, is a full-blooded piece of styling, with a horror of straight lines, even the front bumper being curved. Alongside such a sleek image of power, which offered tempting opportunities for the hyperbole of advertising agents, the Model A seems diminutive and reticent. The potential of standardization to achieve stabilization and continuity of form has here been nullified by the commercial imperatives of the automobile industry.

A similar pattern was to be repeated in many other industries in which mechanisms were mass-produced in highly competitive markets. In some areas of design less susceptible to changes in fashion or exposed to commercial pressures, standardization was to have more complete expression, as for instance in sections of the furniture industry, which was meanwhile undergoing a technological revolution.

A tremendous expansion in the range and capabilities of woodworking machinery had taken place in the United States in the nineteenth century, resulting in new materials that completely altered the nature of furniture production. Timber, in its natural form, is not a homogeneous material; it is rare for a trunk or branch to have a true or consistent straight line; the grain and strength will vary, and it was one of the great skills of traditional craftsmen, such as cabinet-makers, coachbuilders and wheelwrights, to adapt these innumerable variations to their purposes. Mechanical working, in contrast, requires constant dimensions and homogeneous materials to be most effective. By the early twentieth century, timber technology was reaching the stage where new products such as plywood, blockboard, chipboard and hardboard became available in large quantities. Dimensional specifications were devised by national standards organizations, regulating the sizes in which these materials were produced to standard formats, together with quality specifications that indicated their constitution, strength, and suitability for various purposes. The consequences of this process were carried through into the manufactured end-product by an extension of the concept of standardization to embrace three-dimensional form, providing a standard unit of area: a module.

Traditionally, furniture had been produced as separate pieces. A sideboard and cupboard might be linked by means of style and decoration, but they were designed and used as discrete items. A modular system of furniture, however, is composed of a set of units for various purposes which, being

56 The 'Musterring' range of furniture was similar to several other designs produced in Germany in the late 1920s and consisted of compatible units of related dimensions. A range of kitchen units on the same principle, finished in white lacquer, was also offered

designed in multiples of the standard dimensions, are compatible, and capable of being arranged flexibly to suit the space available and the needs of the user. A system of unit bookcases, all four sides of which were interlocking, had been produced by O.H.L. Wernicke in the United States in the 1880s, but it was not until the 1920s that the idea began to have wide currency, when several American and German firms began to market 'combination furniture'. These designs were not modular systems, but rather a series of compatible units that represented a half-way stage. The 'Musterring' range marketed in Germany by Carl Nies of Marburg-an-der-Lahn was typical. Called 'Build-on Furniture', it was sold with the advertising slogan: 'Choose for yourself, furnish for yourself.' It comprised cupboards, cabinets, shelves and bookcases for living-rooms, and did indeed allow a considerable measure of flexibility. The forms of the component pieces were rectangular, with the exception of corner-pieces to link units on two sides of a room; all were designed to fit flush to the walls, and had a polished birch or ivory-lacquer finish. Their simplicity not only matched contemporary taste which had moved away from rich decoration, but can also be seen as a manifestation of the materials and mechanized processes used in their manufacture. Since modern timber-products such as blockboard and

56

plywood are unsuitable for detailed surface working and are most effectively utilized in simple sections, flush unpanelled doors were introduced. Warping is less than with these materials than with natural timber, the planks of which needed encasing in a heavy frame to hold them rigid.

Exactly when the first totally modular system was designed is not clear, but by the 1930s such systems began to appear in many countries. In the Netherlands a full kitchen system was designed for the Bruynzeel company by Piet Zwart. In 1933 Zwart had designed for the firm kitchen cabinets that could be assembled under a continuous working-surface. He realized, however, that it would be more advantageous if kitchen furniture could be produced as a complete package, with standardized units designed for mechanized mass-production. In 1935 Zwart embarked on an intensive study of work in the kitchen and, together with the firm's technicians, produced designs for the 'Bruynzeel kitchen' that went into production in 1938. It was designed to be so flexible that for any surface area, a satisfactory kitchen including a dining area could be built up. Zwart went far beyond most contemporary practice in the range of fixtures and fittings provided in the various units, carefully designing racks, drawers, clips and hooks to accommodate various equipment and appliances. Most systems of the time left a gap for free-standing stoves and refrigerators, but in the Bruynzeel range these, too, were designed as modular units, so that no matter how small or large a kitchen might be, they could be fully integrated. The result, in whatever combination the components were assembled, was intended to be attractive and functional. Zwart later commented that he saw his task as bringing aesthetic quality to add to sober efficiency.

The expansion of commercial and government administration in the twentieth century brought with it voluminous paper-work and documentation, requiring filing and storage, and here, too, modular systems were widely introduced, as being adaptable to all types of accommodation, and expandable according to need. Systems were generally at first of timber construction, but developments in metal-pressing techniques led to the introduction of mass-produced systems of thin steel-sheet office-furniture, of great simplicity and durability, such as the Roneo system. The influence of standardization in this area of design was extended by the introduction of a DIN (German Industrial Standard) specification for a standard system of paper sizes, the 'A-format', in which all sizes of paper products, from postage stamps to large sheets of drawing paper, were multiplications or divisions of a modular dimension, and therefore exactly proportionate. The advantages of this system were so enormous that it eventually formed the basis of an international standard. It facilitated the production of filing systems and paper-handling machinery which could be specifically and efficiently

57 The Bruynzeel kitchen of 1938 by Piet Zwart. One of the most advanced examples in Europe during the 1930s of the use of modular units in kitchen design

58 Roneo pressed-metal office furniture of *c.* 1930, using modular units of filing-drawers which could be adapted to different designs, as in the Midland Bank head offices in London

59 Körting and Mathiesen of Leipzig produced a wide range of functional lighting equipment for industrial and commercial use, such as these photographic copying lights of 1922. Functional form, though with a more detailed aesthetic treatment, was later adapted to the production of domestic lighting

designed to accommodate it, without waste of space or unnecessary complexities.

The severe geometric form of these office systems reflected the utilitarian approach to their design, an impression reinforced by the colours in which the metal systems were offered, usually battleship-grey or olive-green. They provided but little scope for expression, though considerable attention was often devoted to the design of details, such as handles and information-coding. It was an approach that rejected display, however, in favour of a more self-effacing aesthetic of efficiency.

The ideal of efficiency, so vigorously pursued in the early twentieth century, stemmed largely from the work of F. W. Taylor, already mentioned in the previous chapter. It found full expression in the 'rationalization movement' that attempted initially to co-ordinate all stages of production on the basis of detailed time-and-motion studies. At worst, it was an approach that subjected workers to the unrelenting rhythm of the production line, so mercilessly satirized by Charlie Chaplin in the film *Modern Times*.

Many companies came to recognize, however, that uncritical adoption of such methods was counter-productive; that continuous, concentrated work in de-humanized surroundings caused physical and psychological fatigue, thereby impairing efficiency. In the 1920s the rationalization movement therefore sought to create more comfortable and pleasant and hence effective working procedures and conditions. The problem of lighting in offices and factories, for example, received detailed attention, leading to the evolution of new and serviceable forms. Frank and Lilian Gilbreth discussed the new emphasis in their book *Fatigue Study* of 1916: 'Good appearances have always been a large element in making sales, and it is natural and right that the manufacturer should like his product to be attractive in appearance, and that the manager should take pride in the looks of his factory or office. But our entire standard of what is desirable in "good looks" in a work place has changed. We now look for efficiency and fatigue elimination rather than for decoration and glaring polish.'

The refinement of lighting technology and intensive scientific studies resulted in the 1920s in a new generation of lighting fixtures that distributed *59* light evenly, sometimes using opalescent glass covers to reduce glare, and were firmly fixed to walls, or suspended from ceilings by metal tubes that encased the flex, to prevent draughts swinging the fittings and affecting the constancy and distribution of illumination. The German firm of Körting and Mathiesen produced a large series of such fittings in its 'Kandem' range. *81* Another widespread type was for more specific focusing for machine, workbench and desk work. Usually with a spun metal shade, this type had a variety of devices for providing a flexible and adjustable arm. Although not

60 The Terry 'Anglepoise' by
George Cawardine of 1934

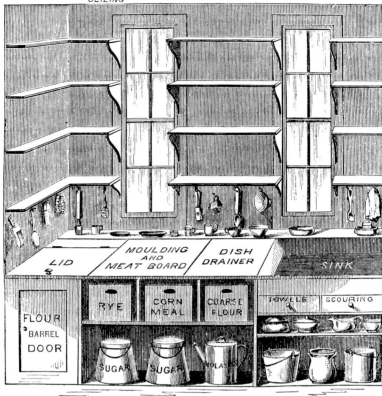

60   one of the first of this type, the 'Anglepoise' lamp by Terry and Co. is certainly one of the most durable, having been in continuous production with little modification since 1934. Its jointing is based on the human arm, and gives an infinite range of possible adjustments over a wide arc.

Posture and comfort in seating were also investigated in detail, leading to considerable improvements in adjustable chairs to give adequate support and more efficient working positions. During the First World War the American Posture League offered standards for posture to anyone interested in improvement. At the same time in Britain, the Medical Research Council began to investigate occupational disabilities, and the Industrial Fatigue Board the conditions for optimum production, amassing by 1930 over fifty reports that provided basic information for designers.

The concept of rationalization was also applied to domestic work, with consequences for structure and form. As in so many instances, the pioneer work stemmed from the United States. In 1869 Catherine Beecher and her

80

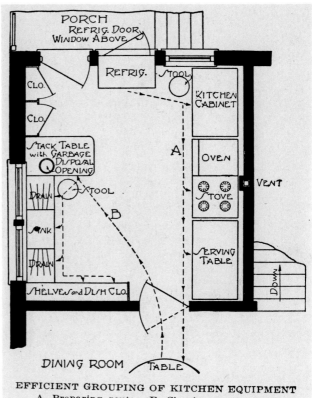

PORCH
REFRIG. DOOR.
WINDOW ABOVE.

CLO.

CLO.

STACK TABLE
with GARBAGE
DISPOSAL
OPENING

DRAIN

SINK

DRAIN

SHELVES and DISH CLO.

REFRIG. STOOL

KITCHEN
CABINET

A OVEN

STOOL

VENT

STOVE

B

SERVING
TABLE

DOWN

DINING ROOM TABLE

EFFICIENT GROUPING OF KITCHEN EQUIPMENT
A. Preparing route. B. Clearing away route.

61 Drawing of grouped sink and food-storage area from Catherine Beecher and Harriet Beecher Stowe, *The American Woman's Home*, 1869

62 Diagrams illustrating the principles of rationalization applied to kitchen work from Christine Frederick's *Scientific Management in the Home*, 1920

sister Harriet Beecher Stowe had written a book suggesting extensive changes in the organization and layout of kitchens, taking the ship's galley   61
with its compact and convenient arrangements as a model. In 1912 Christine Frederick began to apply scientific management methodology to the study   62
of household work. Her writings were very influential in Germany, where the rationalization movement was pursued with particular enthusiasm.

In 1921 the German government founded the Reichskuratorium für Wirtschaftlichkeit (State Efficiency Board) to investigate and publicize more efficient means of production and procedure. It investigated such matters as lighting, working positions and the co-ordination of work-processes – proposing, for example, a uniform method of book-keeping adapted to all sizes of business concerns, so that books and documents could be manufactured more cheaply on the basis of the DIN A-format, with corresponding standardization of document storage and filing. The RKW also devoted many studies to domestic rationalization, producing

63 Cast-iron stoves by Ferdinand Kramer for Buderus, 1931. Such compact designs replaced the large, traditional tiled-stoves used for domestic heating in Germany

64 A bathroom set of 1927 by Ferdinand Kramer for Buderus of Hirzenhain. The form of the bath was designed for a seated posture, requiring less space, an important consideration in design for the 'minimum-existence dwellings' built to rehouse slum-dwellers in Frankfurt in the 1920s

65 The Frankfurt Kitchen by a team under Grete Schütte-Lihotsky was heavily influenced by Christine Frederick's ideas on the rationalization of household work and the forms of galleys on ships and railway dining-cars.

specifications for household furniture and implements to facilitate easier cleaning, washing and cooking, proposing standard sizes for beds and bedding, and defining the most safe and efficient handles for cooking utensils. Each object brought under consideration was analysed under the headings: material, form, function, utilization and price. Inexpensive booklets such as *Household Work Made Easy* and *Standardization in the Home* were published to explain and illustrate these ideas.

It was in the city of Frankfurt, however, that standardization and rationalization found their most complete expression in these years. As a result of the cessation of building-activity in the First World War and the post-war economic depression, enormous social problems faced the city, such as huge slum-areas, deprivation and disease. In 1925 Ernst May was appointed City Architect and embarked on a rapid programme of housing construction. Cost limitations and the urgency of the situation led to a concept of the 'minimum-existence dwelling' as the central feature of the programme, in an attempt to provide rapid improvements in basic living-conditions for the maximum number of people. A careful study was made of household work and dimensions, and since the furniture designed to fit the more spacious pre-war houses was too large to be utilized, a set of 'Frankfurt Standards' was devised to match the new concept. A team of architects and designers including May, Adolf Meyer, Ferdinand Kramer, Mart Stam and Franz Schuster designed new forms of every kind of fitting and furnishing,

63–5 from door-handles to stoves, and even a complete 'Frankfurt kitchen'. Because of the size of the programme, contracts were placed with large firms for their mass-production. Christine Frederick's book *The New Housekeeping* was 'our Bible', according to Ferdinand Kramer. The standard furniture and fittings that he designed were all of the greatest simplicity, but well

65 planned and detailed, and inexpensive. The kitchen designed by a team from the City Architect's office was conceived as a total standard unit to provide an efficient working environment in the minimum space, with built-in storage space and continuous working surfaces. It was spartan, but thoughtfully organized and effective.

Political changes in the Council in 1930 marked the end of the experiment. The achievements of the Frankfurt team, however, with the untiring support of the then Bürgermeister, Ludwig Landmann, were remarkable in the short period of time that was available to them, clearly demonstrating that standardization could be applied to the service of social programmes as well as to the needs of industry.

Frankfurt was an exception, however. In the 1920s, standardization and rationalization came to be regarded as concepts relating solely to industrial and commercial efficiency, and as such, they came under heavy criticism from many groups and individuals. Their contribution to increased production was recognized, but efficiency alone, and the austere aesthetic in which it was manifested, were felt to be inadequate to satisfy human needs. All too often, people were reduced to ciphers in de-humanized environments and processes. Consequently, a shift in emphasis occurred. 'Optimum' instead of 'maximum' efficiency became the goal, resulting in more flexible interpretations. The basic principle remained unaffected, however, and standardization, with its extension into modular units and their incorporation into working systems, remains a fundamental design concept, and one of the most widespread determinants of aesthetic form in modern industrial production.

CHAPTER FIVE

Art and industry in the early twentieth century

At the same time as ideas on standardization and rationalization were evolving, a series of European art movements, such as Futurism, Purism and Constructivism, attempted to redefine aesthetic form and its function in relation to industrial civilization. Although at first sight these two developments might appear antithetical, one based on the pressures of industrial production, the other on artistic theories and values, there is often a striking similarity in the concepts and terminology that each adopted. When employed in different contexts, however, ideas such as 'standards' and 'economy' could assume widely divergent meanings and values.

Paradoxically, the roots of many important elements in this process of aesthetic re-evaluation can be traced to the anti-industrial philosophies of John Ruskin and William Morris. In Britain, their influence resulted in an aversion to industry, and in the Arts and Crafts movement with its advocacy of pre-industrial values. In Europe, although the British critique had wide currency, the anti-industrial stance was modified, eventually becoming transformed into an acceptance of mechanization in pursuit of aesthetic and social ideals. In formal terms, the change was marked by shift of emphasis from decoration and ornament to structural and functional elements.

Although concerned with standards of craftsmanship rather than with industrial production, the Art Nouveau movement of the 1890s, particularly in the *Jugendstil* variant of Germany and Austria, was an important stage in the transition to functionalism. While its development in France, Belgium and Italy was characterized by the use of abstracted natural forms, with a sinuous power of line and three-dimensional moulding that blended the constituent elements of a design into an integrated whole, in Germany it was to take a different course. In Munich, in the work of artists and designers such as August Endell, Herman Obrist, Peter Behrens and Richard Riemerschmid, the flowing curvilinear elements were at first subdued and controlled, and later transmuted into formal compositions of geometric elements. This development became more rigorously stylized in Vienna, where Josef Hoffmann, a leading exponent, became known as *67* 'Quadratl' or 'Right-angle' Hoffmann. The spare angularity of the extensive range of perforated iron-sheet artefacts he designed, dominated by a rectangular grid, show the nickname to have been entirely appropriate.

85

66 Henry van de Velde's workshop at Uccle near Brussels, *c.* 1898

In general, Art Nouveau artists reacted against the diversity, or, as they saw it, the confusion of their times. They rejected the use of past forms and attempted to create a new, universal style which would harmonize all aspects of the visual environment into a total entity, a complete work of art that would be the embodiment of cultural and social unity.

At the heart of the Art Nouveau movement, however, there was an essential dilemma that prevented the realization of these aspirations. This was exemplified in the work and writings of Henry van de Velde, an outstandingly able and versatile Belgian. His writings can seem prophetically modern, citing transport vehicles, bathroom fittings, electric lamps and surgical instruments as 'modern inventions which attract by their beauty', and advocating rationality in design and mass-production. In the

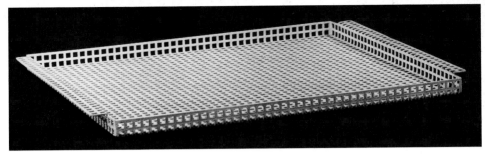

67 Josef Hoffmann, tray of perforated sheet-metal painted white, 1905

context of his work, however, his rationalism did not exclude ornament, but meant, rather, its 'rational' use to express an object's nature and purpose. His concept of the factory was the large craft-workshop he established near Brussels in 1898, and 'mass-production' meant repetitive craft production. *66* He was strongly influenced by Ruskin and Morris, and although discarding their overt nostalgia for the past, sought to develop their moral and social principles, arguing that objects could not be considered separately from the processes of production and utilization, and that artists must be controlling influences to ensure the predominance of human needs. It was for this reason that he established his own workshop, a move paralleled in other centres, in Munich with the Vereinigte Werkstätten, and in Vienna with Hoffman and Koloman Moser's Wiener Werkstätten. Craft production meant, though, that Art Nouveau designers faced the same dilemma as William Morris: their products, of high quality, were expensive and accessible only to wealthy patrons.

Van de Velde emphasized that if artists concerned themselves solely with new forms, these could be exploited out of context, and in this his fears were realized. Art Nouveau designs were widely adopted for industrial mass- *68* production as one style among many to satisfy current fashionable taste – for example, in pressed-metal holloware by the Würtemburgische Metalfabrik in Germany and in Royal Doulton pottery in England.

68 Royal Doulton tea-service decorated in Art Nouveau style, *c.* 1910

From 1900 Van der Velde worked in Germany, later becoming a leading figure in an organization formed to reconcile art and industry: the Deutsche Werkbund. The foundation of the Werkbund in 1907 resulted from contacts between a variegated group of designers, industrialists, journalists and officials, united in their concern for standards of German design. The trend of their thinking was indicated in 1906 in an article by an author and politician Friedrich Naumann, who stressed the need for a new approach to meet the problems posed by industry. 'In the craftsman three activities, of artist, producer and salesman, are combined,' he stated, but since the applied arts were ceasing to be synonymous with handicrafts, these three functions had become separated, and it was therefore necessary to find common ground. This implied a change in attitudes and a need for co-operation. Above all, he argued, a new aesthetic must be sought, since to reproduce mechanically designs for the hand would impoverish the potential of machines. 'This inferior art must be refined, the machine must be spiritualized' and used 'as an educator of taste'.

The foundation document of the Werkbund developed this theme, stating its purpose as 'the improvement of professional work through the co-operation of art, industry and the crafts, through education, propaganda and united attitudes to pertinent questions'. The aim was not just to improve aesthetic standards: 'the validity of artistic standards is intimately linked with the general cultural aspirations of our time, with the striving for harmony, for social decency, for united leadership of work and life'.

The hopes for 'united attitudes', however, were short-lived. The membership, though invited, was exceedingly diverse; and moreover, a sharp ideological polarization developed around the two figures of Hermann Muthesius, an architect by training, and Van de Velde.

From 1896 to 1903 Muthesius had been attached to the German Embassy in London to observe developments in English architecture. On his return, he was appointed to a post in the Prussian Ministry of Commerce with responsibility for applied art education. A catalytic figure in the formation of the Werkbund, he exerted considerable influence by virtue of his extensive experience and government position. For him, the meaning of applied art was simultaneously artistic, cultural and economic. New forms were needed, he argued, not as an end in themselves, but as 'the visible expression of the inner driving force of the age'. Their purpose was 'not only to change the German home and German house, but directly to influence the character of the generation'. Forms therefore entered the field of general culture with the task of expressing the unity of the nation. An artistic style expressive of national culture was, moreover, of economic value: 'Commercial success marches in step with ruling inner values', and, as in France over long periods,

69

69 Hermann Muthesius, interior of Hamburg-Amerika Line pavilion, at the 1914 Werkbund Exhibition, Cologne, with simple Neo-classical proportions and forms

with great cultural qualities it becomes possible, he argued, for a country 'to assume leadership in the applied arts, to develop its best in freedom and to impose it on the world at the same time'. The aesthetic means of establishing a national culture, he declared, was the definition of 'types', or 'standards', to bring about 'a unification of general taste'. Muthesius' use of this terminology is interesting. As a government official he must have been aware of the Prussian system of technical standards, and although his emphasis differed, being on cultural, formal standards, the rationale and justification are very similar.

Van de Velde was less sanguine about the possibilities of uniting art and industry for national economic advantage. To unite the two, he argued, was to blend the ideal and reality, resulting in the destruction of the ideal. He was sceptical about industry's capacity to accept an approach which discounted the value of material success, and reiterated his earlier moral standpoint, that: 'Industry must not think that this idea of beautiful work and of the good qualities of materials can be sacrificed in favour of an increase in profits. We will have no kind of responsibility for objects that pay no attention to

70 Richard Riemerschmid, cutlery designed for Peter Bruckmann and Söhne, Heilbronn

perfection, to the materials used, and that are carried out without pleasure in work.'

In 1914 there was a confrontation at the Werkbund Conference in Cologne, Muthesius submitting a memorandum summarizing his ideas, which was vigorously countered by Van de Velde. After an impassioned debate and vote, Van de Velde's group won a large majority, and the memorandum was withdrawn. Most of the membership still considered themselves artists, and Muthesius' emphasis on formal standards and commerce was interpreted as a threat to their independence and integrity.

The basic problem of the Werkbund was its inability to resolve the breach with industry, and its failure to develop a precise programme regarding form and the role of designers. Apart from Peter Behrens' work for AEG and commissions from two shipping companies, the large industrial concerns remained unaffected by Werkbund activities. Most of the businesses that commissioned members were moderately sized, and often their owners themselves were members, like Peter Bruckmann, the foundation-president,

72 Alfred Grenander, tram-
interior for Berlin elevated
tramway, *c.* 1914

who employed Richard Riemerschmid to design cutlery for his family firm   *70*
at Heilbronn. Karl Schmidt, another founder-member, had earlier set up a
craft establishment at Hellerau near Dresden, which in 1906 amalgamated
with other similar establishments to form the Deutsche Werkstätten under
Schmidt's directorship. Riemerschmid, who was his brother-in-law, later
joined him, and together they established an excellently equipped factory,
part of which was fitted for handwork, but the greater part for the serial
production of furniture and small prefabricated houses. The bed-sitting-
room fitted with Riemerschmid's 1907 designs for what was designated   *71*
'machine furniture' was typical of Hellerau's successful mass-production
series: undecorated, with plain elements, and flush, veneered surfaces. The
Delmenhorster Linoleum Fabrik of Bremen also employed Werkbund
designers, commissioning Van de Velde, Peter Behrens and Josef Hoffmann
to design patterns for production under its 'Anker' brand name. Another
active and versatile designer-member was Alfred Grenander, who executed
many commissions for the Berliner Möbelfabrik, one of the leading
furniture companies of the time, and later designed stations and rolling-stock
for the Berlin elevated tramway. A design by Grenander for a tram-interior   *72*
illustrated in the 1914 Werkbund Yearbook showed a coherent unity and

91

71 Richard Riemerschmid, bed-sitting-room for the Deutsche Werkstätten,
Hellerau, 1907

excellent detailing, the curved seat partitions and upright supports unobtrusively set back to leave the central aisle clear, creating, with the large windows, a light and spacious effect. A major Werkbund exhibition at Cologne in 1914 showed many vehicles in the transport hall, including a railway dining-car designed by August Endell, whose kitchen and serving areas had features that were to influence apartment designs in the post-war period, such as built-in floor- and wall-cupboards, and continuous working surfaces. Walter Gropius' sleeping-compartment designs for Mitropa carriages similarly demonstrated maximum utilization of limited space.

73

In 1916 the Werkbund in co-operation with the Dürerbund, a cultural organization linked to Ferdinand Avenarius' journal *Kunstwart*, published the *Deutsche Warenkunde*, a booklet containing recommended designs for domestic items such as tea and coffee sets, glassware and kitchen equipment. These were generally characterized by restrained decoration, functionality and efficiency, and prices that made them accessible to a wide section of the population. The *Deutsche Warenkunde* was the first of many such publications to attempt to define and publicize standards of design.

During the war the Werkbund organized a series of exhibitions in neutral countries that were essentially propaganda exercises, and from this time onwards became more inward-looking. The internationalist elements of its thinking gave way to a pragmatic acceptance of the economic status quo, and an emphasis on design as a means of improving national economic performance. The evolution of German industry into large, market-oriented organizations was an important factor in this trend towards eliminating programmatic elements and emphasizing the commercial advantages of design.

In painting and sculpture, the comparative freedom of artists allowed a more rapid realization of avant-garde ideas. A notable feature of the artistic movements of this period is the range of fundamental concepts that they share. Despite different emphases and national contexts, there existed a set of characteristics that were international, such as a widespread rejection of 'art for art's sake' and a strong emphasis on the social role of art. This involved a rejection of individual subjectivism, and attempts to place the creation and understanding of art on an objective, even 'scientific', basis. Underlying this tendency was the influence of idealist philosophical traditions, and the search for Platonic ideal forms symbolizing a reality beyond the fleeting changes of the external world, manifested in the trend towards abstraction and, in particular, towards geometric forms. The equation of these forms with machine aesthetics enabled them to be depicted as simultaneously 'timeless' and uniquely 'modern'. The Cubist movement in France was initially of crucial importance in stimulating the development of these ideas. In the

73 Walter Gropius, sleeping compartment of Mitropa carriage, *c.* 1914. The compact efficiency of such accommodation was to influence apartment design

phase of Analytical Cubism from 1909 to 1913, Picasso and Braque began the abstraction of naturalistic subject-matter, which in the subsequent phase of Synthetic Cubism tended more strongly towards geometricization linked to machine aesthetics. An understanding of art came, however, to depend less on its relationships to the external world as perceived by a viewer or user, and more on the interpretation offered by the artist. It was to become evident that such interpretations were not always as objective as was often claimed.

The anonymous utilitarian object was promoted to the status of a 'work of art' by Marcel Duchamp, when in 1914 he bought an inexpensive wire bottle-rack, signed it and displayed it in his studio, asserting that it was art, because he said it was art. Later, in America, he displayed a snow shovel and, arousing outraged protests, a urinal, which he submitted to the 1917 Society of Independent Artists' Exhibition in New York. His purpose was to question the nature of art; but in presenting his so-called 'readymades', he brought them within the compass of his concept of art as a mental act that could not be limited to specific forms and techniques.

Second only to Cubism in influence was the Italian Futurist movement. Founded by Filippo Marinetti, it amounted to a furious and provocative attack on the weight of tradition and a ringing call for Italy to enter the modern age. Modernity meant machines and technology: 'a roaring car that seems to ride on grapeshot is more beautiful than the Victory of Samothrace', wrote Marinetti in the first Futurist Manifesto of 1909. The dominant artistic principle was 'dynamism', which sought to depict the speed, movement and simultaneous sensations of modern life. However, theory and propaganda, art as activity, were at least as important as finished works. The glorification of violence and aggression, of war as a cleansing agent, had a bitter fulfilment in the holocaust of the First World War, when the destructive potential of modern technology was clearly revealed.

The influence of Futurism was mainly in the realm of ideas, and its image of machines transforming society and art was diffused and absorbed across Europe. An important link with Cubism was created by Gino Severini. During an exhibition of his work in Paris in 1916, he came into close contact with members of the Parisian avant-garde, especially Amadée Ozenfant, as a result of which he rejected dynamism, and began to emphasize the machine in terms of function and efficiency, a static ideal of precision and harmony. 'The process of constructing a machine is analogous with the process of constructing a work of art,' he wrote in 1917.

Severini's ideas were taken further by Ozenfant and the architect Le Corbusier, who endeavoured to develop a vocabulary of pictorial elements, combining Platonic idealism with notions of mechanization and modernity. They called their system Purism, and their theories were elaborated in a journal they founded in 1920, *L'Esprit Nouveau*. They propounded a hierarchy of basic geometric forms, and scales of colour controlled compositionally by laws based on the Golden Section ratio, which also determined the geometric proportions, that in turn were related to each other by a modular system.

Le Corbusier was primarily responsible for expressing these theories in terms of architecture and design. The theories of Purism were based on a concept of man as a human mechanism perfected by the processes of natural selection, and functioning according to laws of 'economy'. This perfection was mirrored by those functional objects made by man which corresponded most closely to this same law. Hence the definition of the house as 'a machine for living in', a perfectly functioning mechanism to provide for the utilitarian needs of man. Those objects which most completely satisfied

74 Le Corbusier, interior of the 'Pavillon de l'Esprit Nouveau' at the Exposition Internationale des Arts Décoratifs, Paris, 1925

human needs were designated 'type-objects', the culmination of a process of functional perfection and standardization. In sum, the relationship of man and machine was defined as a response to immutable laws, leading to an aesthetic of classical order and clarity.

In 1925, at the Exposition Internationale des Arts Décoratifs in Paris, Le Corbusier embodied these ideals in the 'Pavillon de l'Esprit Nouveau'. *74* Squeezed on to a cramped site, this was a small house intended to make maximum use of the space available, and, by utilizing to the fullest possible extent standardized mass-produced components and fittings, to provide an image of the possibilities of modern living. The structural frame, the walls, windows and floors, were all of standardized units; the metal doors were produced by Roneo, the office-furniture firm; the fitted cupboards and units all corresponded to a modular system which regulated and unified the proportions. The furnishings were of 'type-objects' such as Thonet bentwood furniture and a table supplied by a manufacturer of hospital equipment. With this pavilion, and the dissemination of his ideas through

75 Gerrit Rietveld, 'Red, Blue and Yellow Chair', 1918. Originally built of plain timber, this better-known version was painted in accordance with De Stijl colour-theories

76 Gerrit Rietveld, interior of the Schröder House, Utrecht, 1924

the medium of *L'Esprit Nouveau,* Le Corbusier became a towering figure in the international art movements of the 1920s.

In Holland, the De Stijl movement, founded in 1917, was similarly based on an idealist philosophy that sought an art embodying a new vision of modern life. In the work of De Stijl artists such as the painters Theo van Doesburg and Piet Mondrian, and the architects J.J.P. Oud and Rob van t'Hoff, there was a gradual refinement leading to a total geometric abstraction. Their ideas were influenced by those of Mondrian's friend the Theosophist M.J.H. Schoenmackers, a mystic and mathematician who stressed the mathematical order of the universe. Formal composition became restricted to the fundamental elements of the horizontal and vertical line, the three primary colours, red, blue and yellow, and the three primary non-colours, black, white and grey, which, they believed, underlay all visible reality. They sought to compose these conflicting elements of line, plane and colour into an image of equilibrium and proportion, as a symbol of the universal harmony of life. The equation of geometric forms with machine production, seen as a means of extending this harmony throughout the visible environment, lent a strong social-utopian emphasis to their theories. 'Art . . . develops forces of sufficient strength to enable it to influence all culture, instead of itself being influenced by social relationships,' asserted Van Doesburg.

A year after the De Stijl group's foundation, Gerrit Rietveld was introduced to it. Trained as a cabinet-maker, and subsequently as an architect, Rietveld was dramatically affected by the contact. In that same year

he created the famous 'Red, Blue and Yellow Chair', one of the first tangible   75
expressions of De Stijl ideals, made of machined wooden laths and plywood
sheets, laid on or alongside one another, screwed together without joints or
rebates, and painted in primary colours. It was a fundamental structural
redefinition of the chair, without precedent. Rietveld continued to
experiment with designs for buildings, furniture and fittings, an exploration
of the De Stijl aesthetic culminating in the Schröder House at Utrecht in   76
1924, when a fortunate commission enabled him to create a total image of
modern living. The functional organization and formal elements of the
house and its complete furnishings and fittings were fused into an integrated
environment, with spatial flow and interplay of lines, planes and colours.

'Avant-garde' ideals seemed for a time to have the greatest possibility of
attainment in the new Soviet state that displaced the tradition-bound Tsarist
regime in Russia. Before the First World War, the Suprematist group
centred on Kasimir Malevitch had moved towards a total geometric
abstraction, with a complementary theory that sought an objective visual
vocabulary, based on metaphysical values attributed to materials and
structure. The October Revolution of 1917, with its promise of a new society
and a new man, was welcomed enthusiastically by the avant-garde, who
generally, and somewhat naively, equated the possibilities of political and
artistic revolution.

The fulfilment of these aspirations, however, was not to be so
straightforward. A debate ensued as to which should take precedence: the
production of agitation posters and objects for use, or the creation of abstract

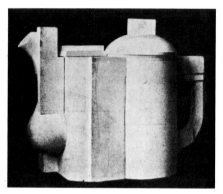

77 Kasimir Malevitch, cup and teapot for the State Pottery, Leningrad, *c.* 1920

structures as models for a revolutionary art. The two viewpoints depended upon two different interpretations of 'function': one emphasizing external utilitarian use; the other, based largely on Malevitch's theories, stressing 'economy' in aesthetic construction. Malevitch's interpretation is illustrated by his pottery-designs of *c.* 1920. Practicality and user requirements are ignored, and 'function' is abstracted to an aesthetic principle of formal economy.

In 1920 Alexander Rodchenko and Varvara Stepanova published a 'Production Manifesto' that attempted to relate the rejection of tradition and enthusiasm for technology to Communist ideology. Their theories of what later became known as Constructivism equated the rational organization of materials with a definition of Communism as 'optimal organization'. The artistic manifestations of these theories were abstract sculptural constructions that explored the concept of material efficiency. Heavy criticism of this 'laboratory art' and its lack of social relevance led to discussions on ways of relating art to industry.

Several theories on this subject had appeared, but these had merely outlined an abstract relationship between art as material construction, a form of work, and factory-work. In 1922, a prominent theorist, B. Arvatov, made a detailed review of industrial work and concluded that production-engineers' work was similar to that of artists, the engineers also being 'the discoverers of things, the organizers of materials, the workers of form' – skills which arose from practical experience, alone the means of discovery and invention. Artists, concluded Arvatov, had broader, more differentiated experience and could therefore replace production-engineers. The work of the proposed 'engineer-artist' was specified by Alexey Gan as twofold: to design both industrial-experimental products and items for mass- and serial-production.

This emphasis on the dominant synthesizing role of the individual engineer-artist was attacked by N. Tarabukin as irrelevant to the nature of industrial production based on the division of labour. Tarabukin was an enthusiast for rationalization, which was a powerful movement in the Soviet Union, being seen as a means of revolutionizing life and work. As leader of the artistic workshops of the Moscow Proletkult organization, he set up a 'Scientific Organization of Work Circle' to investigate the 'rationalization of artistic work which up to now has existed in a chaotic, bohemian condition'. His rationale stemmed largely from Malevitch's principle of economy, which stressed the efficient use, not only of materials, but also of time. By establishing a technical and scientific foundation for art, it was possible to integrate art with society as an element of collective life. In reply, Arvatov continued to advocate the engineer-artist, on the grounds that 'socialism is not a group of homogeneous beings, but an organized unit of

78 Multi-purpose furniture designed under Alexander Rodchenko at the Moscow Vchutemas, c. 1926

highly specialized personalities in collective production'. For him, the role of the engineer-artist was 'the accomplishment of experimental work in model plants and the discovery of standard forms of the material environment'. These standards should not simply be technical specifications, but rather a means of demonstrating standards of collective, socialist life, influencing thought and social relationships.

The practical problems involved in implementing these theories were daunting. Model plants simply did not exist; the only centres for experimental three-dimensional work were the metal- and wood-workshops of the Moscow teaching institution, the 'Vchutemas'. In these, under the direction of Rodchenko and El Lissitsky, strenuous efforts were made to develop methods of production-design, regardless of shortages of materials and equipment. Work was concentrated on designs for standard types of multi-functional furniture. While the frugal simplicity of the forms and the economical use of space well reflected material shortages and scarcity of accommodation, many of the designs still had an air of unreality. Convertible furniture was designed for aircraft and long-distance buses at a time when such forms of transport were virtually non-existent in Russia; and neither the structures nor the materials used were related to existing production facilities. Once again, the gulf between aesthetic concepts and the social conditions of production and use aroused sharp criticism.

The only notable success in realizing standard designs was achieved by the 'Art Circle of Working Youth' (IZORAM), a group of Leningrad industrial workers who designed furniture for workers' clubs and houses of culture, institutions intended as focal points for the development of social and cultural life. Extensive use was made of timber, and of simple forms that were easy to manufacture. From 1928 onwards, tables, chairs, couches and cupboards were produced, an example widely cited of a proletarian art, originating from the masses rather than handed down from professional artists.

The harnessing of all Soviet energies and resources for Stalin's programme of industrialization, introduced with the first Five Year Plan of 1928, brought to an end the years of debate and experiment. That practical results had been few, and production-artists had ended in a no-man's-land that was neither art nor technology, is undoubtedly attributable in part to the parlous condition of Soviet industry, which during the 1920s, after years of war and privation, provided few opportunities for innovatory ideas. But perhaps the ultimate reason for failure was the continuing inability of the avant-garde to relate their utopian ideals and designs to the realities of their time.

In Germany, the belief that art and life could be reconciled by abstract artists creating universally relevant forms for industry came to be identified, above all, with the Bauhaus, the teaching institution founded at Weimar in 1919 following the amalgamation of the art and craft schools under the directorship of Walter Gropius. In the 1920s it was the focus of enormous publicity, arousing enthusiasm or opprobrium depending on one's point of view, and its closure by the Nazis in 1933 earned it a kind of institutional canonization that has only recently been questioned.

To attempt to disentangle the web of myth and actuality surrounding the Bauhaus would require a separate volume, but two aspects of its reputation require consideration here: the first is the claim that the method of education evolved there was uniquely appropriate to industrial design; the second, that the institution is to be regarded as the fountain-head of modern industrial design.

In the early years of the Bauhaus, the stress was placed on uniting art and craft. The foundation of the educational structure was the Vorkurs, or preliminary course, initially developed by Johannes Itten, and compulsory for all students. It emphasized learning by doing. On a basis of theoretical studies, practical work explored and combined form, colour, material and texture. There followed workshop training in a selected discipline of art, craft and, from 1924, architecture, in which the basic Vorkurs method was applied to the chosen specialist activity.

Under Itten the emphasis was metaphysical: on experiment as a means of self-discovery. After his departure in 1923, the Vorkurs was taken over by Lazlo Moholy-Nagy and Josef Albers, who stressed technical objectivity and economy, maximum effect with minimum effort, resulting once again in abstract, geometric form supported by a Platonic idealist theory.

This change reflected a development in Gropius' ideas, with his advocacy in 1923 of 'art and technology: a new unity'. What this actually meant was summarized in a document entitled 'Principles of Bauhaus Production', written in 1926: 'The Bauhaus workshops are essentially laboratories in which prototypes of products suitable for mass-production and typical of our time are carefully developed and constantly improved.

'In these laboratories the Bauhaus wants to train a new kind of collaborator for industry and the crafts, who has an equal command of both technology and form. To reach the objective of creating a set of standard prototypes which meet all the demands of economy, technology and form, requires the selection of the best, most versatile, and the most thoroughly educated men who are well grounded in workshop experience and who are imbued with an exact knowledge of the design elements of form and mechanics and their underlying laws.'

Gropius' terminology needs to be examined in the context of Bauhaus practice in order that his statement may be evaluated. The Bauhaus

79 Marianne Brandt and Hein
Briedendiek, bedside lamp for
Körting and Mathiesen, 1928

'workshops', for example, remained craft-based, and the experience gained
in them bore little relation to industrial practice. The Bauhaus concept of
'standards' differed similarly from the industrial concept, Gropius using it in
the same sense as Muthesius and Le Corbusier, as a cultural type defined in
terms of aesthetic form. Gropius' ideas of economy and form linked to
underlying laws display the tendency to aesthetic abstraction evident also in
contemporary art movements. This is hardly surprising, for the Bauhaus was
a meeting-ground of many of the ideas and personalities already discussed in
this chapter. Gropius and Le Corbusier had worked together under Peter
Behrens; El Lissitsky visited the Bauhaus in 1921; and Vassily Kandinsky,
leader of the Vchutemas painting course, left Russia in 1922 to become a
Bauhaus teacher. Theo van Doesburg from Holland was also a visitor in
1921–2.

   If the results of Gropius' policy are assessed in terms of Bauhaus prototypes
actually put into production, the results are quantitatively insignificant.
Marcel Breuer and Mies van der Rohe developed a series of designs for
80 tubular steel furniture, produced by Thonet and Standard Möbel of Berlin,
that exploited the structural qualities of the material to produce very original
and widely imitated forms; Marianne Brandt and Hans Przyembel designed
79 lights for Schwintzer and Graff of Berlin and Körting and Mathiesen of
Leipzig; Gerhard Marcks, Marguerita Friedlander, Otto Lindig and others
had ceramic-designs produced by several firms, including the prestigious
Staatliche Porzellanfabrik in Berlin. The Adler Cabriolet designed by
Gropius appeared in 1930, after he had resigned from the Bauhaus, but it
illustrates his approach to design. It was an expensive vehicle, constructed in

80 Marcel Breuer, tables of 1926, and cantilever chair of 1928 by Thonet

limited quantities by coachbuilders using craft methods. Its severe geometric emphasis was modified by the rounded edges of the bodywork. Though it was large and stately, the rear end was poorly handled, with, literally, a trunk for storage: a large box resting on a protruding frame. The integration of such elements was becoming commonplace in production cars, but neither this example, nor the technical advances introduced by Ford, nor the ideas on streamlining developed in Germany in the previous decade, find any recognition in Gropius' work.

In sum, the list of industrial products emanating from the Bauhaus was hardly sufficient in range or accomplishment to warrant sweeping claims regarding its significance. In the context of the overall development of design in one of the world's leading industrial nations, moreover, Bauhaus products appear no more than a miniscule contribution from an avant-garde fringe group.

Its educational significance, in contrast, has been enormous, its methods forming the basis of art education in institutions the world over; though the history of its most notable successors, the New Bauhaus at Chicago, and the Hochschule für Gestaltung at Ulm in Bavaria, again cast doubt on the appropriateness of Bauhaus methods as a preparation for industrial design.

The New Bauhaus, founded in 1937, and later incorporated into the Illinois Institute of Technology, owed its existence to the indefatigable

81 'Kandem' hanging lamps by Körting and Mathiesen, 1930. Several Bauhaus members contributed to this range

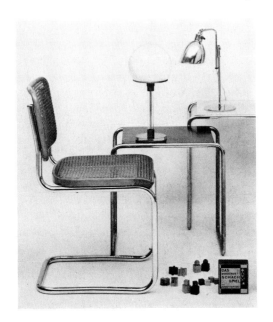

commitment of Lazlo Moholy-Nagy and his wife Sybil. Established as a direct successor to the Bauhaus, it brought a new dimension to creative education in the United States. Yet, as was later pointed out by the journal *Industrial Design*, most of its alumni were employed as artists, craftsmen and teachers, and not as designers in industry.

The Hochschule für Gestaltung, Ulm, was inaugurated in 1955, largely as a result of initiatives by Max Bill, its first director and a former Bauhäusler. Its early existence was scarred by deep controversy between Bill and his deputy, Tomàs Maldonado. Bill had conceived of Ulm as an institution for 'promoting the principles of the Bauhaus'. Maldonado argued that those principles could only be realized by abandoning Bauhaus methods; the emphasis on new forms was irrelevant; instead it was necessary to formulate principles and new methodologies which would enable designers to cope flexibly with the complex demands of technology and industry. Bill failed to gain adequate support among the staff and resigned as director, to be succeeded by Maldonado.

Whatever reservations may be expressed about the Bauhaus, the fact of its enormous influence is undeniable. The varied community of talent gathered together by Gropius was highly individualistic, but developed, too, a strong corporate identity. When scattered by emigration from the Third Reich, the members of this community carried with them a deep sense of conviction that had a profound impact wherever they worked and taught, and was re-affirmed by large numbers of students and adherents. What the Bauhaus was, appears to have been less important than what its members and followers believed it to be. Its influence, far greater than the sum of its practical achievements, is above all a testimony to the power of ideas.

A central belief of the avant-garde movements described in this chapter, and the motivation of their endeavours, was that an artistic transformation of the human environment would, in itself, effect a qualitative improvement of life. The problems of the world around them were thus translated into aesthetic terms, to be shaped and reworked by the power of artistic creativity. It was a process of abstraction, and the results were frequently esoteric, comprehensible only to a small, like-minded group. The new forms that were evolved, though often of great imaginative force, were assigned a utopian role and value that were rarely self-evident, and were difficult to sustain. Consequently they often seemed to have little relevance to the problems they purported to solve, and were widely received with incomprehension and hostility. Complex social problems, it became clear, could not be solved by formalistic aesthetic means alone. The belief that artists and designers were the transformers and legislators of human society was a compelling ideal, but they were a parliament without an electorate.

CHAPTER SIX

The emergence of professional industrial design

The First World War stimulated an enormous expansion of America's productive capacity, which was converted after 1918 into a consumer boom. With the growth of mass-production, based on massive capital investment, there was a constant search for means of reducing costs and increasing sales. Standardization and rationalization, improved production methods and new materials could do much to reduce unit costs, while an emphasis on visual form became an important instrument to boost sales, not least because, with the growth of advertising, the visual image was frequently more widely diffused than the product itself.

In 1927, however, a recession began to set in. Many small firms went bankrupt or were taken over, accentuating the trend towards larger combines. The Wall Street Crash of 1929 and the Depression that followed created intense competitive pressures among those firms that survived.

It was in this economic context that a new generation of industrial designers emerged. They came from diverse backgrounds, and their methods and achievements were very varied, but as a result of their work, design came to be recognized as an essential feature of commercial and industrial activity, a specialist element within the division of labour implicit in mass-production and sales.

Many industrial designers came from a background connected with advertising and presentation, such as commercial art, exhibition and display, or from stage design, and were accustomed to working in a commercial context, often as part of a team, and to taking decisions requiring the reconciliation of competing claims. From this background, too, designers adapted the organization and methods of the consulting agency, working for a variety of clients.

The process of adaptation that took place is well illustrated by the work of Walter Dorwin Teague, a successful graphic artist who began to experiment with three-dimensional design in the mid-1920s. In 1927 he was commissioned by Eastman Kodak to design cameras and packaging, and in 1928 introduced a fashion element with the 'Vanity Kodak', the body and bellows of which were produced in a range of colours with chrome-plated metal trim, and that had a matching silk-lined case. His subsequent work shows a growing regard for technical factors. The 'Bantam Special' of 1936

82 was a small hand–held camera reduced to basic elements for ease of use. The horizontal metal strips on the case appear at first sight solely decorative, but were raised from the moulded body to limit the surface area over which the lacquer coating had to be spread, thereby reducing the danger of chipping and cracking. Teague's ability to resolve technical problems in terms of aesthetic form established a working relationship with Kodak that lasted throughout his life. When the company set up its own design department after the war, he advised on its formation and continued to act as chief consultant.

Other early work by Teague was the design of office machines for the American Sales Book Company, and of Heald heavy industrial machinery. In each case, he worked with company engineers, reducing a clutter of gears, levers, screws, slots and protuberances to a cleaner, unified form that not only looked more attractive, but by focusing on essential working parts and controls, made them easier to use. As a result of such work, his commissions constantly expanded in size and scope.

Raymond Loewy was a Frenchman who after war service left for America, establishing himself there as an illustrator and display designer. In 1929 Sigmund Gestetner asked him to redesign a duplicating machine, giving him five days for the task. A visual simplification was all that was possible in so short a time, but Gestetner, impressed, commissioned Loewy to redesign later models fundamentally. These designs, too, concentrated on combining improved appearance with increased operating efficiency. Loewy's 'Coldspot' refrigerator of 1935 for Sears, Roebuck provided a dramatic demonstration of the impact of design on sales. Earlier refrigerators

82 Walter Dorwin Teague, Kodak 'Bantam Special' camera, 1936

83 Raymond Loewy,
'Coldspot' refrigerator
designed for Sears, Roebuck,
1935

had been monumental in appearance, set on high, curved legs, and had the
cooling-unit exposed. Loewy encased the whole in a plain, white-enamelled   *83*
steel box with a flush door. Its chrome hardware was intended to have a
jewel-like quality, set off by the stark background. The interior was carefully
designed to accommodate containers of different size and shape. It had a
semi-automatic defroster, instant-release ice-cube trays and a glass rolling-
pin that could be filled with ice-cubes for improved pastry-making. The
model set a new trend in refrigerator design, and annual sales soared from
15,000 to 275,000 within five years.

Loewy's practice also grew rapidly. By 1947 he had seventy-seven clients,
spanning buildings, shop-fittings, product design, transportation vehicles
and equipment, and packaging.

Henry Dreyfuss' background was stage design, but in 1929 he changed
direction and opened an industrial design office. In the following year, he
was one of ten artists offered one thousand dollars by the Bell Telephone

84 Henry Dreyfuss, '300' type desk set, 1937, for Bell Telephones

Company for ideas on the form of future telephones. Dreyfuss was convinced that speculative designs of external form alone were irrelevant, and therefore declined, insisting on the necessity of working with Bell's engineers and designing 'from the inside out'. The company felt this process would limit artistic scope; but it changed its mind when the submitted designs were found to be unsuitable, and commissioned Dreyfuss to work in the way he wanted.

Since a telephone service was not subject to market pressures, new apparatus had to be justified by improved performance and lower operating costs, and required a form that would not date rapidly. Bell had first introduced a handset, designed by company engineers, to replace upright models in 1927. In 1937, this was superseded by Dreyfuss' 'Combined Handset', produced initially in metal, and from the early 1940s in plastic. Intended to be unobtrusive and suitable for use anywhere in homes and offices, it was therefore reduced to essential elements. Meticulous preparatory studies and tests in use ensured that it was easy to operate. The simplicity of the moulding facilitated cleaning and servicing, and minimized the possibility of damage. On the strength of this design Dreyfuss was appointed consultant to Bell, working for many years on all their products, which in 1950 comprised more than one hundred pieces of apparatus.

At the core of Dreyfuss' success was his belief that machines fitted to people will be the most efficient. Over many years he assembled data on the human body, its proportions and capabilities, which he summarized in 1961 in his book, *The Measure Of Man*, that helped establish ergonomics as an essential tool of designers. The influence of these studies was demonstrated in a range of tractor designs for the John Deere company, developed from 1955 onwards, and in earth- and materials-moving and road-building machines for Hyster, all built around a comfortable, ergonomically-calculated

84

working-station for the driver. For the external forms of the vehicles a clear, balanced composition of volumes created an impression of solidity and efficiency.

Teague, Loewy and Dreyfuss were all based in New York, but Chicago was also an important centre where many designers, such as Dave Chapman, Jack Little and Peter Muller-Munk, developed extensive practices. The 'Century of Progress' exhibition of 1934 was a key event, employing many young exhibition and display designers who progressed into industrial design through the experience and contacts they gained there. Typical was Jean Reinecke, who opened a partnership with Jim Barnes in 1935 and built a large client-list. Reinecke's most enduring design was also one of his smallest: a dispenser for Scotch Tape. With hundreds of imitations, it has become so commonplace, and its principles so obvious, that the ingenuity of the original conception is easily overlooked.

The American furniture industry was a notable training ground for professional designers. By the early twentieth century it had attained a level of mechanization and mass-production ahead of the world, and many firms established studios, from which designers such as Gilbert Rohde and Donald Deskey branched out into other fields. One of the most versatile was Russel Wright, who trained as a painter and designed for the theatre before turning to furniture. His 'American Modern' range was mass-produced by Conant-Ball from 1935. Made of solid bleached maple, it comprised co-ordinated

85

85 Russel Wright, 'American Modern' dining-room furniture produced by Conant-Ball from 1935

items for all parts of the house, unified by the overall use of plain, rectangular volumes, with rounded edges of wide radius, and large, emphatic, handles as the only decorative element. In the year it appeared, Wright formed a partnership with Irving Richards, a businessman with an enthusiasm for modern design. Wright's dream of redesigning 'everything for the world around us' was balanced in the partnership by Richards' grasp of the importance of marketing, summed up in his comment, 'A design is as good as the entrepreneur who promotes it.' Wright designed a series of oven-to-table-ware in spun aluminium for the company, followed by lamps, also in aluminium, and a range of ceramic dinner-ware, all under the label 'American Modern', and characterized by unembellished forms that emphasized the quality and finish of the materials used.

The styling departments were large employers and also important training grounds for designers, who were often able to extend their range of activity as automobile firms moved into other areas of production. General Motors, for example, acquired a refrigerator company, renamed Frigidaire, in 1919. (When asked to explain this move, the then President, Will Durant, laconically pointed out that both automobiles and refrigerators were boxes containing a motor.) In 1936 a smaller car-producer, Nash, merged with Kelvinator, a domestic appliance firm; and when Sears Roebuck set a design department for its vast range of products, the members were recruited from Detroit, mainly from General Motors.

In 1928, Harley T. Earl was appointed head of the new Art and Colour Section of General Motors, and in 1938 this department expanded to become the Styling Section, when it employed three hundred people, a clear indication of its importance. As chief stylist for what was to become the world's largest industrial conglomerate, Earl came to exert enormous influence over the appearance of modern industrial products, and was a key figure in establishing a new role and status for designers in corporate organizations.

The agencies established by consultant designers varied considerably in size. Dreyfuss in New York had a staff of about fifteen, and limited the number of clients he had at any one time. Loewy, in contrast, had several offices in America, and others in Britain, France and Brazil, employing hundreds. Most principals employed specialist staff in areas such as engineering, market-research and model-making. This level of organization accounts to a large extent for the amazing quantity and diversity of work they produced. Egmont Arens, for example, was credited by 1938 with the design of over a thousand items, a testimony to the rapidity with which designers became accepted. Their success has occasionally been attributed to the flamboyant manner in which some marketed themselves, but, more

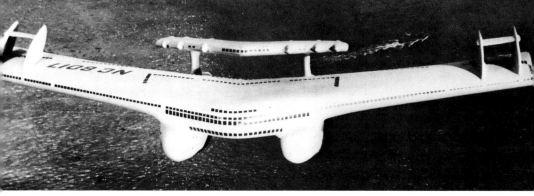

86 Norman Bel Geddes, model of projected 'Aircraft Number Four'

fundamentally, it hinged on their ability to adapt their creativity to commercial disciplines.

An exception to the general adaptability was Norman Bel Geddes, who began as a stage designer. Some of his early designs were very successful, but he was an idealist who tended to disregard public demand and the limitations of production techniques. His friends thought him a genius, but his critics accused him of wasting more of industry's money than anyone, or anything, else. He was at his best when his futuristic vision was allowed full play, as in his pavilion for General Motors at the New York World Fair of 1939. A lack of commissions and above all his own financial mismanagement caused his agency to collapse shortly after the Second World War.

He was important, however, for a book, *Horizons*, published in 1932, that had considerable influence. His enthusiasm for technology was linked to a dynamic concept of progress, and an ideal of creating a life for everyone that through technical advance would be materially improved and aesthetically enhanced. *Horizons* included a series of futuristic projections, speculative designs for aircraft, ships and cars whose proposed size and speed became realizable only some forty years later. Smooth, organic shapes, like that of 'Aircraft Number Four', were integrated and unified by rounded forms and *86* sweeping lines. Bel Geddes was not the inventor of 'streamlining', as it became known (see following chapter), but he did much to popularize the style.

Although there were parallels with the United States, the pattern of development of the design profession in Europe was not entirely similar. Divergent conditions and attitudes provided different opportunities or constraints. Although consultant designers in the American sense hardly existed until after the Second World War, the possibilities of industrial design were extended, generally within the more specialized working context customary in Europe.

One of the most notable German designers committed to mass-production was Wilhelm Wagenfeld, a former Bauhaus pupil and teacher who came to reject the ideas of that institution as theoretical and self-centred. Designing in industry, he declared, was a co-operative act, and had little in common with the working methods of artists. He repudiated function as a determinant of form, arguing that it was not an end-purpose, but a precondition of good design. This re-orientation of his standpoint, and his undoubted skill in adapting to industrial production, enabled him, unusually for a former Bauhäusler, to continue working as a leading designer in the period of the Third Reich.

In 1929 Wagenfeld began to obtain commissions from industry for furniture, porcelain and Jena glass, the success of this early work leading to his appointment in 1935 as artistic director of the Lausitzer Glasverein, with a brief to improve quality at all levels. His fine glass for exclusive lines received international acclaim, but most of his work was in pressed glass, for which he designed hundreds of inexpensive items, wine and beer glasses for restaurants and bars, bottles and jars for commercial use, domestic glassware, and a modular system of kitchen containers and dishes, including his 'Kubus' range. All were unadorned, relying on clean lines and subtly curved forms that exploited the ductile qualities of glass with restraint. After the war he became an independent designer, his commissions including cutlery for the Würtemburgische Metalfabrik and some excellent electric light fittings for Lindner of Bamberg, in which the stark geometric shape of the light-globes was modulated by more organically shaped plastic casings housing the electrical connections.

87

87 Wilhelm Wagenfeld, 'Kubus' modular glass containers designed for the Lausitzer Glasverein in 1938

88 Walter Maria Kersting, radio-cabinet in moulded plastic, 1928

Less well known than Wagenfeld, but an important pioneer of industrial design in Germany, was Walter Maria Kersting, who, in his designs and teaching, sought to integrate considerations of aesthetic form with commercial and technical factors. In a book, *The Living Form*, published in 1932, he described the role of designers as the creation of 'simple and inexpensive objects, that should not appear more than what they are. That can be purchased everywhere. . . . Capable of being produced in series in craft workshops and mass-production factories.' Mechanisms should be simple, he argued, in order for them to be immediately comprehensible to a non-mechanically minded person, and foolproof against mishandling. This approach was manifested in his design for a radio–cabinet of 1928, that in concept, form and materials was remarkably innovative. The moulded plastic casing which integrated the component units of the radio, and the clarity and simplicity of the controls were features that were later widely adopted in commercial production. Kersting's opposition to the Nazi regime prevented adequate recognition of his abilities until after the Second World War, though it did not prevent the government from using his radio design as the basis for the 'Volksempfanger' (Peoples' Radio), an inexpensive standardized radio produced with government sponsorship as a propaganda instrument. Kersting's versatility and inventiveness belatedly found expression in the 1950s, in a wide range of designs, including lighting and cooking appliances, telephones, sewing machines, and industrial machinery and electrical equipment.

88

89 Alvar Aalto, chair of bent plywood for Paimio Sanatorium, 1928

In many European countries, architects frequently found opportunities to work in industry and made major contributions to design. In Finland, Alvar Aalto began experiments with furniture in the late 1920s, and in 1935 became a partner of a firm called Artek, which produced his designs. These utilized laminated birch and plywood sheet for forms which were a fascinating combination of constructivist and organic ideas, austere in structure, but softened by curved forms and the warmth of the polished timber.

One of the most active and versatile architects to work in the field of design was Gio Ponti. In 1928 he became editor of the magazine *Domus*, through which he had great influence for many years on design in Italy. He developed a concept of 'true form', to be attained by discarding all conventions and remoulding a form in accordance with its function, though this remained a method of approach, and never hardened into a deterministic style. His work spanned ceramics, metalware, lighting, furniture, and domestic and commercial fittings of many kinds. From the mid-1930s he

114

90–1 Gio Ponti, washbasin stand
and lavatory bowl for Ideal–
Standard, 1954

designed furniture for the Figli di Amadeo Cassina firm. One of his most successful pieces for them was a chair, 'La Superleggera', first produced in 1955, a subtle and delicate composition of slim tapered elements, slightly angled to fit the body. In contrast, his gleaming chrome-plated coffee machine for La Pavoni in 1949 was more assertive and imposing, becoming a key icon of the coffee-bar cult that swept Europe in the 1950s. A further example of his versatility was a set of sanitary ware for the Ideal-Standard Company, exhibited at the Milan Triennale of 1954. This included a slim washbasin stand and a lavatory bowl set high on a plinth to emphasize the forceful sweep of its lines. These established a trend for the design of these items. The dramatic sculptural shape of the lavatory bowl roused an American critic, who had doubtless read Marinetti's manifesto, to liken it to the Winged Victory of Samothrace, and it is interesting to speculate on what Marcel Duchamp's reaction would have been.

90–1

The flow of ideas and designers between countries in the inter-war years meant that most innovations soon had international currency. The ideas of the Bauhaus, for example, were brought to Britain by Walter Gropius and Marcel Breuer following their emigration from Germany in 1934. They were welcomed by a group of Bauhaus enthusiasts, including Jack Pritchard, who had earlier worked for Venesta, a company importing plywood goods from Estonia and Finland, for whom he had engaged Le Corbusier to design an exhibition stand. Pritchard had subsequently established his own furniture production company, Isokon, for which Breuer designed some excellent models, such as his elegant long-chair. This was intuitively formed to fit the human body in a reclining posture, and the open wave-like form of the chair surface was counterpointed by the taut, compressed angles of the laminated-timber frame. Other cosmopolitan influences in Britain at that time were Wells Coates, born in Canada, and Serge Chermayeff, of Russian extraction, also architects who had turned to design, producing both original radio-casings for Ecko and designs for studios and offices for the BBC. Gropius, Breuer and Chermayeff all left for the United States in the late 1930s, feeling that the atmosphere there was more open to innovation, and contributing to what continued to be a two-way flow of influences across the Atlantic.

The influence of the Arts and Crafts tradition in Europe remained strong, and was adapted to industry. In Britain, Gordon Russell, at the height of his career as designer and maker of fine craft furniture, changed direction, and with his brother R.D. Russell, designed mass-produced radio-cabinets for the Murphy company. The impetus for this change of direction, as with many American designers, came from the Depression, which caused a drastic reduction in furniture orders from the United States. The Russells' designs used bent plywood-sheet, a far cry from expensive natural timbers, but they 92 showed great skill and ingenuity in devising forms appropriate to mechanical production that displayed the same sensitivity to materials and form as did their more exclusive craft products.

In Scandinavia, industrialization came late with electrification, and the handwork tradition was reconciled to industrial methods by a succession of 'artist-designers'. Wilhelm Kåge, for example, joined the Gustavsberg china factory in 1920, and was able to combine the creation of highly individual artistic stoneware with designs for the quantity production of table-services, kitchen and sanitary ware. In Finland, the team of artists gathered by the Arabia Company in the 1930s under Kurt Ekholm produced a similarly diverse range, while the glassworks of Karhula-Iittala employed two outstanding figures in Timo Sarpaneva and Tapio Wirkkala, and also produced designs by Alvar Aalto. The most remarkable example, however, of the influence of artist-designers was the Orrefors Glass Company. Simon Gate was appointed in 1916 and Edvard Hald in 1917, the first of a string of outstanding talents employed by the firm, who established high standards across the product-range. In 1933 Hald was appointed managing director, a clear recognition of the importance design had assumed for the company. In the 1950s the mass-production glassware of the firm gained world-wide popularity, the table set by Nils Landberg of 1957 epitomizing the simple, 93 yet subtle, forms characteristic of their popular series.

92 Gordon Russell, bent plywood radio casing and matching table for Murphy Ltd, 1930

93 Nils Landberg, glass service-set 'Illusion' for Orrefors

Designers had traditionally worked in glass, ceramics, furniture and metalwork, but what was remarkable in Scandinavia was the way individual artistic development was widely linked to industrial methods to produce quality goods, to the extent that Orrefors' serially-produced wares were frequently sold in craft shops. After the Second World War, a large body of creative talent was available in Scandinavia capable of adapting to the new industries that emerged. Sigvard Bernadotte, for example, designed fine silverware for the Georg Jensen company, and also, together with Acton Bjorn, Facit office-machinery and office-furniture systems for Åtvidabergs. Sixten Sason trained originally as an artist in Paris, then as an engineer, a background that admirably equipped him to combine the treatment of aesthetic and technical factors. His designs included domestic equipment and power tools for Husquarna and vacuum cleaners for Electrolux, and he was consultant on the modular system for Hasselblad camera apparatus. Sason also developed a close working relationship with the SAAB company and was responsible for the external and interior designs of their cars from the first model, the '92' of 1950, with its aerodynamic lines revealing the influence of the company's origins in aircraft production. Finally, he conceived the outstanding '99' saloon, produced shortly after his death in 1969, that combined a finely proportioned body with an interior that was both efficient and comfortable.

94

A great many other designers of outstanding ability emerged to prominence in the years before and after the Second World War, and the sheer volume and range of their work makes generalization very difficult. It was, however, just these qualities of diversity and versatility, an ability to work in terms of solutions to specific problems in varied contexts, rather than generally imposing stock forms or stylistic devices, that made them so successful. By the 1950s, there were few firms of any size or repute, in industrial countries, that did not recognize the significance of the pioneering work of the inter-war years by employing professional designers, either directly or as consultants.

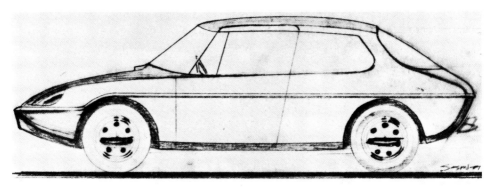

94 Sixten Sason, sketch for SAAB '99' saloon, c. 1960. The concept of a wedge-shaped car was very advanced for its time

CHAPTER SEVEN

The introduction of streamlining

The intense commercial competition created in America by the Depression, described in the previous chapter, gave rise not only to a more professional approach to the design of products, but also to a style, streamlining, that has come to stand uniquely for dynamism and modernity.

Streamlining was popularized by the visionary designer Norman Bel Geddes to the extent that it has sometimes been considered synonymous with American industrial design of the 1930s and 1940s. Although some designers were irritated by this stylistic tag, streamlining was in fact extensively applied to industrial products, sometimes on the basis of scientific calculation, but often for its symbolic properties and without functional justification. A classic example of the latter was the Hotchkiss stapler designed by Orlo Heller in 1936, claimed to be 'the most beautiful stapler in the world'. It was a piece of pure styling, of mannerism imposed with little attention to mechanical function. The dominant horizontal rearward curve of the shell led away from the stapling lever at the front, which operated on a vertical axis: a form that expressed speed applied to a static object. Yet the emblem of speed and modernity was a powerful symbol, and did not necessarily impair the efficiency of an object, even if it did not express its function. Streamlining on this level became tremendously fashionable, to the extent, according to one story, that a coffin manufacturer asked a designer for his latest in streamlined caskets.

Such excesses should not obscure the real achievement of streamlining, however, which, in the work of some engineering designers, powerfully

95

95 The Hotchkiss stapler, 1936

96 Douglas DC2 airliner entered by KLM in the 1934 London to Melbourne Air Race. Carrying a load of passengers and mail, it came second, its sophisticated organic form heralding the era of regular long-distance passenger services

synthesized aesthetics and technology. Its origins can be traced to nineteenth-century studies of natural life, and an appreciation of the efficiency of organic form in fishes and birds. These ideas were to be applied to submarines and airships, both evolving to a long, slender shape, pointed at the front to improve penetration, and tapered at the rear to reduce turbulence and 'drag'.

By about 1900 the 'teardrop' had been accepted as the form of least resistance. This form was chosen intuitively for car designs by the Italian coachbuilder Castagna in 1914, and the German aircraft-designer Edmund Rumpler in 1921. A turning point was reached in 1921 when Paul Jaray, a Hungarian engineer at the Zeppelin works in Friedrichshafen, began to test streamlined automobile models in the company's new wind-tunnel. The forms he evolved profoundly influenced European car design in the inter-war years, providing scientific justification for streamlining in terms of increased speed and stability.

In aircraft design, innovations in metals technology, construction techniques and scientific studies contributed to a revolution. Cumbersome box-frame fuselages and heavily braced wings were replaced by integrated, monocoque structures with streamlined, aerodynamic forms.

The first commercial airliner incorporating these developments was the Boeing 247 of 1933, developed from a military bomber. In the same year the Douglas DC1 appeared, designed specifically for commercial use, with an all-metal structure, the wings integrated into the fuselage and a stressed aluminium skin, resulting in a gleaming, integrated form that had a dramatic impact. In the following year, a Boeing and an enlarged Douglas model, the DC2, were entered in the London to Melbourne Air Race, finishing third and second respectively behind a British racing plane specially built for the event, the DH88 Comet. The two American craft created a sensation. Cyril Kay, a pilot in the race, recalled that, 'one glance at their aerodynamically clean lines and handsome, stressed-skin finish was enough to emphasize their advance over all contemporary design'.

96

The culmination of the Douglas design team's work was the larger version of the DC2, the DC3 of 1935. This revolutionized air transport, and some thirteen thousand were eventually built. It became a symbol of the age, a key-object in technical aesthetics, and was even referred to as a work of art. Performance, however, was the basis of its success. When adapted for military use in the Second World War, it became legendary for its ruggedness and reliability under the most difficult conditions.

Wind-tunnel testing was widely adopted for automobiles, and proved that streamlining reduced resistance, giving fuel economies at high speeds. Far-reaching technical and mechanical innovations were necessary, however, fully to exploit the potential benefits. One such attempt at radical change was that of the visionary American architect and designer Richard Buckminster Fuller, in his 'Dymaxion' cars of 1933–4. These were large, three-wheel, teardrop-shaped vehicles for which superior performance and a fifty per cent fuel saving at 50 m.p.h. were claimed. Fuller's sweeping re-appraisal of both form and structure was too extreme for the American automobile industry, however, committed as it was to a concept of mass-production that depended upon judging the willingness of the public to accept innovation.

97

Originality had therefore to be tempered by caution in the design departments established under various titles by the large automobile manufacturers, led by General Motors. After Alfred P. Sloan became head of General Motors in 1923, the company began to whittle away Ford's sales lead. Sloan introduced the annual model change as a competitive weapon, and, realizing the need for closer attention to appearance, appointed Harley T. Earl to design a 'La Salle' car for the Cadillac division in 1927 and then to take charge of an enlarged 'Styling Section'. Although Earl frankly admitted to designing for obsolescence, the stylistic changes he introduced were none the less gradual, with streamlined forms used in a restrained manner, within the accepted public concept of what a car should be. The caution of Earl's approach seemed to be justified by the experience of the Chrysler Corporation. They, too, had begun to take styling seriously, by 1937 employing a hundred people on the work. These designers were members of

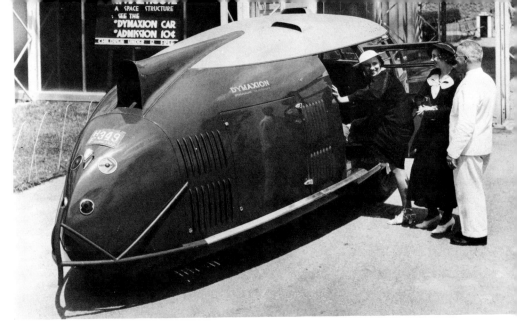

97 Buckminster Fuller with his Dymaxion Car No. 3 at the Chicago World's Fair, 1934. Poor rear vision detracted from its innovatory qualities

the engineering division, however, and in the Chrysler 'Airflow' car, 98 produced in 1934, it was the ideas of Carl Breer, the chief engineer, that dominated. The project was radical in nature, a bold attempt to gain a competitive lead. The structural configuration and mechanical layout were the basis of the design, intended to provide stability and comfort. Considerable efforts were made to unify the body, with the double curve of bonnet and body smoothly linked by the rearward-sloping windscreen, and accentuated by the flowing line of mudguards and running-boards. Although incorporating numerous innovations, and launched with a massive advertising campaign, the model failed to sell. The general feeling was that it was too innovatory, though some critics more contentiously suggested that it was too ugly.

The impact of the streamlined forms that evolved in America was not restricted to that country alone, but was felt across the world, conveyed predominantly through the imagery of publications and films. In some areas, such as Latin America, American economic dominance and heavy imports of American industrial products made it more immediate. In addition the search for wider markets led many American companies to establish or purchase factories in other countries. Ford and General Motors both had subsidiaries in Europe by the 1930s, and adapted Detroit methods of design and production to local conditions.

98 Chrysler 'Airflow' car, 1934. Commercially unsuccessful, but profoundly influential

In some respects there were marked differences between Europe and America. The European contribution to streamlining was not dependent on the American, but developed its own line of research and expression. Paul Jaray's experiments in streamlining, mentioned on page 121, were brilliantly continued by Hans Ledwinka, an Austrian working for the Czech firm Tatra, whose V8 saloon of 1934, with the flow of its lines culminating in a rear fin, was acknowledged as one of the outstanding vehicles of the decade. The new autobahns in Germany also created great enthusiasm for streamlining, and companies such as Mercedes and BMW produced some fine vehicles which balanced streamlining with the more restrained European tradition of bodywork design, as in the elegant BMW 327/18 Coupé of 1937. In contrast to America, these were expensive limited production cars, however, still requiring a high degree of industrial craftsmanship.

It was in the field of European small-car design that the greatest difference was apparent in comparison with America. In the inter-war years the Austin Seven, a sturdy vehicle of box-like proportions in its early forms, set the pattern, followed by such vehicles as the bulbous Fiat 'Topolino' of 1935. The Citroën 2CV, however, was a complete rejection of streamlined styling. Developed by Pierre Boulanger before the war, it was first produced in 1949, with uncompromisingly functional bodywork referred to by some critics as

99

124

99 Tatra V8 car, type 81, designed by Hans Ledwinka, 1934

100 Pininfarina's Cisitalia Coupé, 1947

a product of the 'garden-shed school of auto design'. Its rugged simplicity made it very popular, and supply could never keep up with demand. Another of the most successful post-war small cars was also a pre-war design. In this case, the designer Ferdinand Porsche was a leading exponent of streamlining theory and practice. An attempt to produce a 'People's Car' by American mass-production methods was the basis of Hitler's plans for a small inexpensive vehicle, suitable for use on autobahns. The prototype of the Volkswagen designed by Porsche appeared in 1936–7, but it was not actually mass-produced until after the war, when its beetle-shape became the most widespread example of 1930s streamlined design.

100 In the post-war years a brilliant school of coachbuilders emerged in Italy, with such names as Pininfarina, Bertone, Ghia and Michelotti coming to exert enormous influence both in Europe and America. Pininfarina's 1947 Cisitalia Coupé incorporated considerable technical advances and displayed refinement of streamlined form, the purity and elegance of line being the most striking feature, setting alternative standards against the baroque styles emerging in America. The activities of the Italian coachbuilders divided into two areas: consultancy work for mass-production companies at home and abroad, and design of expensive custom-built models that were mobile pieces of sculpture, occasionally exotic and flamboyant, but serving as a platform for the evolving and testing of new concepts of form.

The domestic consumer goods industries of Europe generally tended to follow the American pattern, though on a smaller scale, introducing formal changes in design as an instrument of competition. In Britain, HMV employed Christian Barman to design a range of electrical products that was strongly marked by the influence of streamlining, for instance an electric iron that integrated handle and body in a curving, amorphous casing, and a convector heater in a pattern of superimposed chrome-plated shell-like forms. Both appeared in 1934. As in America, however, different markets imposed varying demands and altered the emphasis in design. The Swedish telecommunications firm of L. M. Ericson pursued a policy similar to Bell of America, based on technical research and owing little to fashion. Their first handset was produced in 1908, and the 1931 model by Jean Heiberg was a beautifully proportioned plastic moulding. It predated Dreyfuss' set for Bell by six years, and was adopted in many countries.

Streamlining is unique as a style that stemmed predominantly from the conditions of scientific research and industrial production rather than from aesthetic theory. The commercial pressures that had led manufacturers to seize upon it so avidly in America in the 1930s were not to ease, and its diffusion throughout Europe and the rest of the world during the 1930s and 1940s continued in the context of corporate competition.

CHAPTER EIGHT

Corporate design and product identity

If the growth of industrial design as a profession during the 1930s and 1940s was due in considerable measure to designers' ability to adapt their creative talents to the demands of commercial production, it also required, as a corollary, that manufacturers recognize the potential of design and provide designers with opportunities to prove their worth. For many who did so, the incentive was increased sales, with design as a convenient weapon in their annual marketing strategy. Other commercial organizations were less concerned to attract customers at point-of-sale, or by advertising, than to convey a general impression of modernity, quality, service or reliability. Graphic imagery and typography were widely used to develop a house-style or corporate identity, presenting a visually unified image to the public, and in large organizations, to employees as well. Vehicles, machines, furnishings and fittings were similarly capable of use in this context. Company policies regarding design, the forms utilized, and the purposes they were intended to serve were, however, very varied.

In many cases, greater attention to visual identity was a response to pressures of competition. During the inter-war years, the growth of alternative forms of transport, such as motor cars, coaches and aircraft, had caused railways to suffer a serious loss of passenger revenue. In consequence, they updated their approach not only by introducing new forms of motive power such as diesel and electric engines, but also by cultivating an image of speed and modernity. Streamlining was widely used to this end. As with automobiles, there had been early, intuitive attempts to apply streamlining to trains. A fascinating experiment in Germany in the late 1920s was the propellor-driven *Rail-Zeppelin* by Count Kruckenberg, a noted airship- and aircraft-designer. The influence of his background was evident in the slim cigar-shaped body of the vehicle, and its rear propeller. Though unsuitable for general use, the vehicle demonstrated the possibility of adapting to railways both the lightweight body-construction and the diesel engines of airships. These lessons were embodied in the diesel-electric railcars introduced in 1933 by German State Railways: fast twin-units, the first of which, *The Flying Hamburger*, linked Berlin and Hamburg, some 180 miles, in two and a half hours. The design was well integrated and balanced, with front and rear evenly rounded, an enclosed chassis and clean surfaces, the

101

101 *The Flying Hamburger* of German State Railways on its inaugural run in 1933. The vast crowd of onlookers (above) testifies to the powerful attraction of streamlined vehicles in the 1930s

102 Three-car diesel railcar by Count Kruckenberg for German State Railways, 1937

body painted in horizontal bands of purple and cream. A further
102 development, also by Count Kruckenberg, was a three-car unit produced in 1937, with a streamlined torpedo-shape, again showing the influence of aircraft design. This was capable of carrying one hundred passengers in air-conditioned coaches, double-glazed to reduce noise. The outbreak of war, however, prevented its production in quantity.

In Germany and the Netherlands, where some of the finest diesel-units of the decade were produced, streamlining was applied in smooth, organic
103 forms. In contrast, Ettore Bugatti's railcars for the French State Railways were angular, with a wedge-shaped front and rear. The three configurations

103 Railcar designed by Ettore Bugatti for French State Railways, *c.* 1934

104 The Burlington *Zephyr* by the design team of the Budd Manufacturing Company, 1934

of a convex curve on end-surfaces, a torpedo or bullet shape, and a forward wedge, became the predominant formal elements used in railway streamlining.

In America, by the early 1930s, public interest in streamlining was growing and companies raced to produce designs. The Union Pacific led the way, introducing in February 1934 a three-unit train, *City of Salina*, built by the Pullman Company. It was fast, with a low centre of gravity, and powered by a large internal-combustion engine. The interiors, as one might expect from the builders, were comfortable, with double ranks of reclining, upholstered chairs and air-conditioning. The external design, though, was

105 Otto Kuhler's *Rebel* diesel
unit for the Gulf, Mobile and
Northern Railroad, 1935

106 Sir Nigel Gresley's 'A4'
class express locomotive
Mallard for the London and
North Eastern Railway, 1935

uncertain: the front end was bulbous, with a clumsy grill, the rear a graceless spheroid, while lines of protruding rivets and sheet-metal joints broke up the surfaces.

Two months later, to a great fanfare of publicity, the Chicago, Burlington and Quincy Railroad produced a train that had an astonishing impact: the *Burlington Zephyr*. This, too, was an articulated three-car unit, with an innovatory General Motors diesel engine that was light and powerful enough for express-work. The body used a new technique of welding stainless steel, developed by its builders, the Budd Manufacturing Company, to give a strong, lightweight structure. Painting was unnecessary, the polished gleam of stainless steel providing a brilliantly effective finish. The front end was rounded and angled forward, somewhat like an Etruscan helmet in appearance, while the rear had an elliptical observation car fitted with comfortable armchairs. The corrugations running above and below the windows strengthened the car structure and at the same time provided a unifying motif along the length of the train.

The *Zephyr* received over half a million visitors during a six-week-long exhibition tour. It appeared at a time when hope was beginning to revive after the hardships of the Depression, and, as with the DC3 aircraft, its radically new form was a symbol of progress renewed, and of better times to come. There was even a feature film made about it, *The Silver Streak*, with the *Zephyr* in the starring role.

The *Zephyr* had one disadvantage, in that the articulated unit was fixed in capacity and extra cars could not be attached. Subsequent designs solved this simply by reverting to a separate power-unit and detachable cars, unified in form and colour. The first of this type were the *Rebels* of 1935, designed by Otto Kuhler for the Gulf, Mobile and Northern line. Their form was very

assured and crisply detailed, the windows were large and well articulated, the radiator–louvres were tucked away and barely visible on the roof, and the headlamps were recessed to give a smoothly integrated appearance.

Diesel streamliners were an enormous success, and a great many were built. They were fast and efficient, clean and comfortable. Above all, they provided a dramatically new image for the railroads, enabling them to withstand the competition of other modes of travel for some years.

Many companies remained committed to steam, and yet adopted streamlining. The London and North Eastern Railway had, in Sir Nigel Gresley, one of the outstanding locomotive designers of the period. His experiment with new configurations, carried out over many years, culminated in his 'A4' class of 1935 for the high-speed London to Edinburgh *106* run. These were fully streamlined, in profile a convex wedge, and Gresley went to great lengths to ensure the configuration was functionally justified, and not only in respect of performance. The elongated teardrop shape on the side-valancing over cylinders and wheels had a broad step on top to facilitate cleaning. They were fine engines, one of which, *Mallard*, set a world speed record for steam locomotives of 126 m.p.h. in 1938.

Traditional values still had a strong hold, however, and the attitude of railway designers in Europe towards streamlining was sometimes ambivalent. Gresley was steeped in the British practice of deriving a locomotive's aesthetic from its functional elements. Some of his conventional designs were superb, and he could be quite scathing about 'tin-casings'. The German '05' class express locomotives had one of the most comprehensive casings of the time, that almost completely covered the wheels, producing a weighty, curving, biomorphic effect. The Director of German State Railways commented on this design: 'Without a doubt, the aesthetic suffers from the strong casing, for the steam locomotive is, in its form, one of the most beautiful of machines.' He regretfully concluded, however, that 'increased performance could not be sacrificed on the altar of beauty'.

In America, such figures as Teague, Dreyfuss and Loewy were commissioned to streamline engines, in an attempt by various railroads to update their image without taking the radical step of changing their motive power. The results sometimes bore little relationship to the engine's form, but Loewy's 1936 redesign of the Pennsylvania Railroad 'K4' class was a carefully composed bullet shape, based on the cylindrical form of the boiler, that sought to retain the character of a steam locomotive within the streamlined format.

There were many other excellent but less well-known designs from all parts of the world. The South Manchurian Railway introduced a fine Pacific-type locomotive in 1934, built by Kawasaki, a company that was later to become internationally known. The engine's casing was well detailed, and combined a smooth, uncluttered surface with clear access to working parts that needed frequent maintenance, a practicality that was often overlooked.

While the long-distance railway services were fighting to retain passengers, suburban commuter lines in expanding large cities had to cope with constantly increasing numbers, and the resultant need to modernize stock and improve their image. The early steam-hauled trains of the Berlin Stadtbahn, for example, had demanding schedules and were hampered by passenger coaches with nine doors that presented a danger when opening on

107 South Manchurian Railway express locomotive built by Kawasaki, 1934

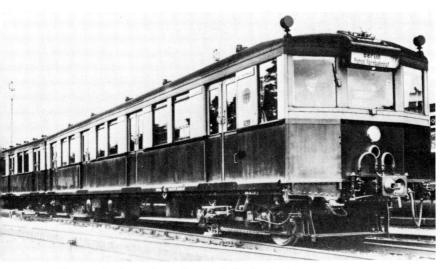

108 'Type 165' railcar of 1927 for the Berlin Stadtbahn

to crowded platforms, and caused delay by having to be closed individually before departure. After the First World War a series of experimental coaches were used to test carriage layouts and sliding doors, and when it was decided to electrify the Stadtbahn, the results were embodied in a standard design. It was also decided that the new units should be designed to look functional, comfortable and attractive, 'in order', said an official, 'to achieve a stronger traffic advertising effect'. Nearly thirteen hundred of 'Type 165' were built *108* between 1927 and 1930 to meet the electrification programme. This was a neat, angular design, finished in two-tone paintwork of Bordeaux-red and beige. The carriage floors were level with the platform, and there was a slight flare at the base of each coach to narrow the gap. Four double sliding doors, manually opened but closing automatically, solved the problem of passenger exchange. Their modernity, in image and fact, compared to the old steam services, was very real.

Many cities also developed underground systems, and for this type of transport, London became a model, with electric trains introduced as early as 1890. The numerous disparate companies that initially ran the system each designed their own stock, but after a process of amalgamation the first of a series of standard units appeared in 1923. This had air-operated, automatic sliding doors and a combination of longitudinal and bay seating, a basic format that was progressively developed.

The formation in 1933 of a unified authority, the London Passenger Transport Board, to control bus and underground services, under the operational direction of Frank Pick, consolidated and extended the progress of the previous decade. Pick was a benevolent dictator who believed it was his duty to educate the public to an appreciation of good design, which, for him, meant order, fitness for purpose, and harmony, expressing practical needs, but also signifying moral and spiritual order. Buildings, graphics and fittings of all kinds, as well as vehicles, were redesigned under his direction. Historical styles were rejected, and an image of modernity was sought in clear unembellished forms, deriving their aesthetic value from a logical and efficient adaptation to function. This approach culminated in the 1937 Tube *109* Stock, with clean exterior lines and flush welded surfaces modulated by the *110* balanced rhythm of windows and doors. The interiors were well proportioned, with upholstered seating and fittings unobtrusively but

109–10 London Underground Tube Stock of 1937, with the clean, well-proportioned lines of the external surfaces, and the characteristic interior layout combining longitudinal and bay seating (below)

efficiently distributed. Motor buses, too, started to be built to standard designs. The 'STL' double-decker series, first produced in 1933, had clearly articulated lines and proportions, avoiding the heavy, box-like appearance of its predecessors by eliminating the peak over the cab, inward-sloping the front and rear ends, and adding a strong curvature to the line of the roof-dome.

Long-distance coach services increased with the construction of better roads. In Germany, streamlined coaches for autobahn services were popular, but were constructed in limited series by coachbuilding firms. The Greyhound Corporation in America, however, bought large numbers of vehicles, and in 1934 commissioned Raymond Loewy to work with General Motors to establish a clear company identity. This was achieved with a unified body-shell in unpainted aluminium-alloy with smoothly rounded edges and a horizontal linear emphasis, and a large leaping greyhound logo to provide unmistakable identification. The 'silversides' coach design was subsequently modified and adapted to many changes of vehicle, while retaining its essential features.

Air transport remained luxury travel in the 1930s, a fact reflected in designs and publicity. Plane interiors, especially those of the giant flying-boats popular at that time, such as the Martin M-130 *China Clipper* of Pan-American Airways, and the Short Empire class of Imperial Airways, had lounges furnished with clubroom-type armchairs, spacious and comfortable dining-rooms with meals cooked on board by a chef, and even a small promenade-area. The expansion of air travel after 1945 meant, however, that aircraft interiors lost their luxury image, evolving as a form of mass-transportation. The huge cost of developing new airliners for this purpose faced designers with often conflicting demands. A reassuring environment and passenger comfort were not easily reconciled with economic pressures to fit as many passengers as possible into a given space. Henry Dreyfuss, working on interiors for the Lockheed Constellation and Electra, undertook considerable research into the ergonomic dimensions of seating to ensure optimum comfort compatible with the spatial restraints imposed.

The pressures to ensure designs were meticulously worked out before production also led to a new scale of experimental modelling. When working on the Boeing 707 in the early 1950s, for example, Teague constructed a complete working interior mock-up, with lighting and sound effects simulating flight, in which 'passengers' were seated for the time-span of prospective journeys, served by the full complement of airline staff. The experiment cost half a million dollars, but many details were improved, and prospective airline purchasers had the opportunity to satisfy themselves of the aircraft's practicability. Teague's design established the pattern of layout that has become a common feature of modern airliners, with ranks of multiple high-backed armchairs.

Teague attempted to mitigate the effects of overcrowding by avoiding unnecessary visual detail. Lights were recessed, and hand-luggage storage, passengers' lighting and ventilation, and emergency equipment were built into continuous panels along the overhead wall. Plastic panelling, upholstery and carpets were in subdued tones. It was essentially a bland and restrained approach, attempting to soothe rather than stimulate.

Many manufacturers of consumer goods looked to designers to help them to establish an image of quality, as with the Scandinavian firms described in Chapter 6 (pages 117–19). An outstanding American example was the furniture company of Herman Miller. When purchased in 1923 by D.J. DePree, this was a typical Grand Rapids firm, producing bedroom furniture in decorative 'period' styles dictated by wholesale buyers. DePree became interested in contemporary design after seeing an exhibition of French furniture, but economic conditions at the time made innovation risky. Around 1929 he met Gilbert Rohde, who prepared for the company bedroom furniture designs of very simple forms, the antithesis of the Grand Rapids tradition; indeed when DePree showed them to his bank manager, the latter commented that it would be madness to produce them. The project was in jeopardy, but Rohde appealed to DePree's religious convictions by arguing that he was not just selling furniture, but a simpler, purer way of life. Fortunately for DePree's commercial and ethical well-being, the new products were highly successful, and the company became strongly established on the basis of the quality of its modern design.

On the death of Rohde in 1944, George Nelson, trained as an architect, but establishing a reputation as a furniture designer, was chosen as his successor. His 'Storagewall' of 1945, produced for a feature in a *Time/Life* publication, attracted great attention. It was a hollow, modular interior wall with flexible shelving, designed as both partition and storage unit, an idea later developed further for Miller in a series of modular storage units and seating, and integrated systems of great flexibility for office landscape-planning.

Nelson's work was excellent, but it was overshadowed by that of a friend, Charles Eames, whom he persuaded DePree to employ. Eames designed *111–113* many products, some for other companies, but his series of chairs for Miller established him as one of the outstanding designers of the century.

By the time of his appointment in 1946, Eames had established a workshop in Los Angeles with his wife Ray, where they embarked on a remarkable series of researches into structures and materials. He experimented with plywood for many years, attempting to mould a chair in one piece, then using separate sections that could be produced more easily. He later turned

136

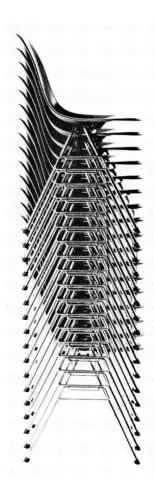

111–13 Charles Eames: (top) dining chair of moulded walnut plywood and steel rods with rubber shock-mounts, 1946; (left) stacking-side chair of moulded polyester and steel tube, 1955; (below) lounge chair of die-cast aluminium and Naugahyde cover, 1958. All produced by the Herman Miller Corporation

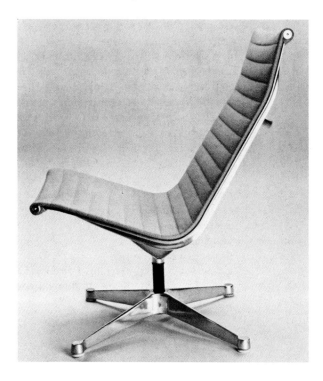

his attention to stamped steel, aluminium castings, fibreglass reinforced plastics, thin-gauge wire and steel rods. What was so impressive about all his work was that the results were entirely individual, yet precisely worked out within the confines of the process by which they would be manufactured. His work was prolific, but three examples will illustrate its diversity.

111 The first model for Miller, in 1946, was a dining chair, the fruits of his earlier experiments with plywood. The seat and back were moulded in subtle curves to provide comfort and support, and set on a chrome-plated steel-rod frame of the utmost simplicity, joined by rubber shock-mountings. All the elements and the connections were precisely articulated, giving the chair a strength and stability that belied its delicate appearance.

112 With his later experiments in moulded polyester, Eames returned to the problem of producing a chair in one piece. His stacking side-chair of 1955 was the culmination of a number of models, and has been imitated so frequently that it has become one of the most widespread types of inexpensive modern chair.

113 At the other end of the price range, a lounge chair of 1958 used die-cast aluminium ribs supporting a gently-angled thin-profile seat, in which the covering layers of fabric and inner sheet of vinyl foam were welded at intervals to ensure stability under the pressure of a reclining body, giving a pattern of horizontal ribs.

In one sense, Eames' workshop perfectly epitomized Gropius' concept of the artist's studio as an industrial laboratory, though for him, technology was no abstraction, but a reality that through years of disciplined and painstaking work he came to command, to a degree that allowed his imagination full play. The mutual co-operation and regard that developed between Eames and the Miller administration and workforce were vitally important factors in enabling him to produce so much that was so good. With his designs, and those of George Nelson and other notable figures such as Robert Probst, the company established a reputation that few could match.

Another example of a design policy based on the encouragement of individual talent, but in a very different context, is the Italian office-machinery firm, Olivetti. Its founder, Camillo Olivetti, designed the firm's first typewriter in 1913, emphasizing that its aesthetics had received particular attention. 'The typewriter', he stated, 'should not be ornate and in questionable taste. It should have an appearance that is serious and elegant at the same time.' It was not until his son Adriano took over, however, that this principle became translated into a defined policy. By 1930 Adriano had overhauled the production organization of the firm, putting it on a sound economic footing, and turned to design, beginning with graphics and advertising. In 1936 Marcello Nizzoli, a well-known graphic designer, was appointed to advise on the casing of calculating machines. He adapted very successfully, and over many years designed a range of products with ever-greater assurance. His two typewriters, the Lexicon 80 standard of 1946 and the Lettera 22 portable of 1950, firmly established Olivetti's international reputation. With the Lexicon, the visible mechanism, usually a clutter of levers, gears, roller and bars, was designed in balance with the bodywork, which had a gracefully rounded solidity.

In the late 1950s other designers began to develop a close working relationship with the company, notably Mario Bellini and Ettore Sottsass. Bellini's work concentrated on electronic adding and calculating machines and office computers, and shows great ability in combining sophisticated technology, operational simplicity and sculptural flair, as with the 'Divisumma 18' calculator of 1969. Sottsass was engaged in 1956 to design Olivetti's first computer, the 'Elea 9003'. This was an austere set of units based on a standard framework, determined by a belief that the aesthetic should emerge from a rationalization of work-processes.

Sottsass' outlook was later modifed by a deep interest in Indian and Far Eastern philosophy, and many subsequent designs were less rigidly rational, though no less functional, delighting in strong colours and plastic forms, as with the Valentine portable typewriter and a co-ordinated set of office furniture and fittings, 'Sistema 45'. Of this, he wrote that a firm producing   *114, 118*

114 'Sistema 45' office furniture by Ettore Sottsass for Olivetti, 1969

machines 'cannot limit itself to the responsibility of the functioning of the machine for what it is, but must pledge itself to assume the responsibility for all the reactions that can arise when machines invade the environment, men and their lives. . . . We thought we should exercise "yoga" on design, liberating shape . . . stripping from it every attribute, sex-appeal, deception.' Sistema 45 sought to overcome the alienation and factory-like atmosphere of many offices, with an environment to which a user could relate as a full human being, with feeling and delight. Its forms were distinctive and solid, combining simple volumes with bright, emphatic colours. Each working detail was defined in terms of its own function, but co-ordinated visually and functionally with other elements, within the overall approach determined by Sottsass. It was appropriate that it should have been designed for a company that, under Adriano Olivetti, developed a social welfare policy based on a recognition of the value of every employee as an individual.

It is interesting to compare Olivetti with one of its main rivals that also instituted a comprehensive design policy: International Business Machines. IBM established a design department in 1943, though consultants were still used, including Norman Bel Geddes, who was retained to design a typewriter, the 1947 'Model A'. He assigned the job to a member of his staff, Eliot Noyes, who had studied architecture at Harvard under Gropius and Breuer. When Bel Geddes' agency collapsed, Noyes completed the Model A on his own account and was retained for further projects. His effectiveness developed through a close working relationship with Tom Watson Jnr, head of IBM. After Noyes had proposed a corporate programme on the lines of Olivetti's to meet the needs of the expanding company in 1956, he was appointed Consultant Director of Design with very wide powers. The pattern he established was a company design department for continuity and basic standards, with outside consultants for fresh ideas, under his own overall direction. He rejected annual model changes and concessions to marketing, scornfully dismissing them as 'all that witchcraft'. IBM set out to create an élite image, and the conformity to the company's standards expected of employees, also extended to design as defined by Noyes. 'There must be consistent use of colour, detail and form – square corners and standard heights, kick-strips, bases and superstructures,' he stated. A set of IBM standards was published, establishing design specifications for all products.

IBM design was closely linked to the company's programme of technical innovation. In 1961, for example, they introduced the 'Selectric' typewriter which typed by means of a 'golf-ball', a moulded sphere bearing the usual characters, numbers and marks that moved across the paper, dipping and turning to present the correct aspect. For this innovatory model, a unified

115 IBM 'System 360' computer designed by a team under Eliot Noyes, 1964

envelope casing emphasized visually the elimination of type-bars and movable carriage, and the simplification of the mechanism that resulted.

Three years later, IBM introduced a new generation of computers, the 'System 360', which used micro-transistors, and was small, compact and very versatile. It consisted of a series of rectangular units on a modular basis, some working-parts of which were left visible to offset their starkness. The control-console was designed in close co-operation with the 'human engineering' section, to be clearly comprehensible and easily operated. As was generally the case with IBM designs, it was an image of technical efficiency. Whether IBM designs were indeed always superior is debatable, but, as Wally Olins commented in his book *The Corporate Personality*, 'IBM products, whether they are office equipment or computers, have a cachet.' Though Olivetti was the example that had inspired Noyes, the role of aesthetics for IBM differed markedly. Whereas Olivetti encouraged individuality, IBM emphasized conformity to its image, which in formal terms, was an extension of the Bauhaus idealist concepts learnt by Noyes at Harvard.

The German firm of Braun, producers of electrical consumer goods, although much smaller than IBM, have also used design as the foundation of a corporate identity programme. In 1951 when after their father's death,

115

116 Braun 'Kitchen Machine KM 321', 1957

Artur and Erwin Braun took over the firm, its products were technically sound but undistinguished. The brothers were interested in modern design and decided on a new approach. With Fritz Eichler as head of design, Braun began to pursue a policy of uncompromising modernity for products aimed at the upper reaches of the market. In 1955 Dieter Rams joined the staff, and was largely responsible, with Eichler and Hans Gugelot, for establishing the formal characteristics of Braun design. These first aroused widespread attention with the 'Kitchen Machine KM 321' of 1957, a composition of simple masses, with clean lines and an appearance of solidity and stability. A series of alignments and parallels created a strong sense of order, as with the line of the bowl-rim continuing the joint in the casing, and the curves of the casing aligned to those of the bowl. Every element of Braun designs was similarly balanced and unified, though this did not always mean a simple symmetry. It was a reductionist approach, eliminating every unnecessary detail, concentrating on ordering essential elements, and reflected, too, in the almost invariable use of white surface finishes, with grey and black detailing.

In many companies, as with IBM, design was linked closely to large 'research and development' departments, its role being to give the latter's

142

work a form accessible and acceptable to the public. An example of this pattern applied to mass-production was provided by the American firm Corning Glass, one of whose best-known products was 'Pyrex' glass oven-ware, first introduced in 1913. Its forms were derived from traditional patterns adapted to modern methods of pressing, and the range sold well as functional and cheap. After the Second World War, however, when its patents began to expire, Corning decided to establish a design department as a means of meeting competition. Their director, Arthur A. Houghton, believed a product had two qualities: 'utility value' produced by science and technology, and 'satisfaction value' created by art and design. The role of the design department was to ensure the second, by making products more beautiful and convenient to use. Redesigning the Pyrex range, the department softened its utilitarian appearance with curved side-walls and edges, the latter smoothly drawn out to form integral handles, and by this means, extended the range's application as oven-to-table ware, while retaining its image of technical quality. In 1953 Corning's research department developed a ceramic-like glass material called Pyroceram that was gleaming white, of fine texture, and capable of withstanding enormous variations of temperature, and in 1958 a range of hugely successful oven-to-table products in this material was marketed under the name Corning Ware, later extended to portable electric appliances such as coffee-makers. While the designs were very different in size and shape, all were characterized by

117

117 Corning Ware as redesigned by Sam Mann and Roland G. de Puy in 1964

simple forms that allowed the material full expression, decorated only by a tiny blue cornflower motif that provided identification.

Packaging is usually integrated into overall graphic corporate identity programmes, but often a distinctive three-dimensional form becomes synonymous with a product, as with the Coca Cola or Haig 'Dimple' whisky bottles. The curved outline of the 'Coke' bottle was developed in 1915 and was later given definitive form by Raymond Loewy, becoming one of the best-known commercial icons in the world. The development of automatic methods of producing glass bottles and jars, and later plastic containers, led to their endless proliferation and opened the floodgates of design-fantasy. The whole area of packaging is a vast one of fluctuating forms and fashions on which considerable time and ingenuity are spent.

While the attitudes and expectations of organizations define the conceptual boundaries within which designs are created, successful innovation still depends upon the skill and ability of designers, acting individually or co-operatively. Integration of the design-function into the structure of companies means, however, that designers' achievements cannot be considered in isolation, but have to be understood and evaluated within the framework of the corporate purposes they serve, and the corporate values they express.

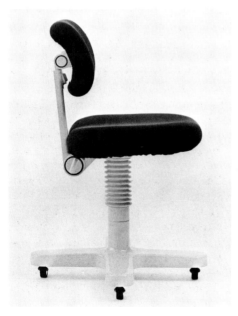

118 'Sistema 45' typist's chair designed by Ettore Sottsass, 1969

144

CHAPTER NINE

Technological innovation and design for the home

The extension of mass-production techniques to the manufacture of domestic implements and appliances, and the widespread introduction of mechanization in the home, have resulted in the modification of traditional forms and the invention of many new ones, in which an emphasis on attractive appearance involved designers to an increasing extent. The cumulative effect of these changes has been to transform the work and functions associated with the life and running of a family household.

One of the most fundamental changes during the last two hundred years has been in fuel and power sources. For centuries an open fire was the means of cooking, heating, and often lighting too. The introduction of town gas in the early nineteenth century separated the use of power from the source of its generation, enabling a greater diversity in the forms and locations in which it was utilized. Cooking and heating tended to diverge, with specific forms developing for each, a tendency accelerated in the early twentieth century with the spread of electricity-generation.

The pattern for modern cooking appliances was established by the gas stove in the late nineteenth century: a free-standing form with a box-shaped oven, usually raised on legs to give easy access, and above it a cooking range with two to four burners. Stoves were usually constructed of cast iron, often with decorative mouldings. In the 1920s, enamelled steel-sheet was introduced, which enabled a lighter structure to be built, with flush surfaces and clean lines, often emphasized by a white enamel finish. In 1932 the Standard Gas Equipment Corporation of New York produced a new design by Norman Bel Geddes embodying influential changes in form and production. An SGE catalogue of 1931 contained models already considerably advanced technically, integrating storage space for utensils and covering the oven and a burner-range with a folding plate to make a 'table-top'. Bel Geddes' design continued this concept, but eliminated supporting bowed legs and the dust-harbouring space beneath the stoves in favour of a plinth, thus creating greater storage space. His designs also aimed at improving the overall appearance, with clean lines punctuated by large heat-resistant handles, and rounded edges. Vitreous enamel sheets were clipped into place on a steel frame instead of bolted on, saving time and reducing the risk of damage in assembly. The most fundamental production change,

119

however, was that around one hundred models, each with individual components, were replaced by twelve standard component units, comprising ovens, burner-ranges and storage spaces, that SGE combined into sixteen models, with considerable savings.

The improvements in the design of gas cookers were consistently innovatory, competing effectively for a long time with electricity. Solid-fuel cookers were never entirely superseded, though, and the 'Aga' stoves developed in Sweden in the 1920s, and the comparable 'Esse' models made in Scotland, were slow-burning, extremely efficient, and could also be used to provide space-heating. The Agas' large size, simplicity, well-balanced volumes, good detailing and light-enamel finish made them a strong focal point in a kitchen.

There were many early experiments in applying electricity to cooking and heating, for example by the firm of Crompton and Company, which in 1891 displayed a number of appliances at the Crystal Palace Electrical Exhibition in London. Shortly afterwards, at the 1893 Columbian Exposition in Chicago, a 'model electric kitchen' was exhibited in which every item utilized electric power. Companies such as Crompton and British Prometheus, and in Germany, AEG, Siemens and Therma, marketed kettles, irons, grills, toasters, ovens and cookers by the mid-1890s, generally in florid, decorative styles typical of the period; they were expensive and not totally reliable, and the high cost of electric power and its limited availability prevented their widespread adoption.

A major problem in Britain and America was that utility companies generating electricity felt little interest in anything other than public lighting, and consequently only operated during hours of darkness. It

119 Gas cooker designed by Norman Bel Geddes for the Standard Gas Equipment Corporation, 1932

required strenuous efforts by appliance manufacturers to convince utilities of the potential in exploiting the full capacity of their plant.

In 1908 A. F. Berry marketed an advanced electric cooker, the 'Tricity', in Britain, and embarked on a programme of public demonstrations and lectures to arouse interest. His efforts were very successful; longer generating hours were introduced in some districts, lower prices for electricity resulted, and utility companies developed profitable business from hiring cookers and selling appliances. Large department stores also began to realize the potential of electricity and ran promotion campaigns, like that of Wanamakers of New York, which in 1906 organized an 'Electro-Domestic Science Exposition' including a model electric kitchen and bedroom.

Many devices were incorporated into early designs, providing a foretaste of the emphasis on gadgetry and convenience that has since become commonplace in appliance design. The 'Nightingall' oven, which appeared in Australia around 1908, had automatic heat-control for a range of temperatures, as did the Copeman Automatic Cooker produced in America around 1911, with the added advantage of a time-switch to turn current on and off at predetermined times. The Copeman had two stamped-aluminium ovens inside an insulated wooden casing set on legs and resembling a sideboard. The clutter of clocks, controls and wiring set on a stretcher between the front legs created a Heath Robinson-ish appearance. As with many early designs incorporating new concepts, it revealed an uncertainty over the form in which innovation should be embodied.

In fact, electric cookers generally followed the forms and production methods established for gas stoves, with greater attention to styling and presentation becoming apparent by the 1930s. Their mass-production in America had results characteristic of the approach to the design of consumer goods in that country. A team from the OEEC European Productivity Agency visited the United States in 1954, and noted that appliances were much cheaper than in Europe, and better value, a standard American four-ring cooker being considered the equivalent of a German 'de luxe' model. They also remarked on the degree of standardization: the Hotpoint company, for instance, produced seven models of one type differing only in minor refinements and accessories, to which the assembly lines could be swiftly adjusted, enabling standard dies and presses to be used to full capacity, thus lowering costs.

Electric lighting was far more convenient and efficient than gas or petroleum lamps and was universally adopted wherever electric current was available. Space-heating devices also increased in popularity, though to nothing like the same extent. In both cases, a reduction in size of the functional elements diminished their significance as direct influences on

147

form. This liberation from functional imperatives led to the production of such appliances in a bewildering variety of designs, corresponding to virtually every style and taste purchasers could desire, with the purist argument that simple, undecorated forms were appropriate to modern technology being generally disregarded. A device that outraged advocates of 'good' design, then and ever since, was the Berry 'Magicoal' electric fire introduced in 1920, which adapted the new technology to the British love of an open fire. Designed to be set in a traditional fire-place, it had horizontal radiant electric heating bars, and above them coloured imitation coals of semi-transparent material, with a flickering light playing across the underside, simulating a real fire. The surrounds were produced in a range of styles, some of them cheerfully indiscriminate blends of several periods. It remains enormously popular and widely imitated, a testament to the persistence of social habit in the face of change.

The foregoing examples were all of age-old functions adapted to and transformed by electrification, but refrigeration, as a domestic necessity, was without precedent. The speed of its diffusion in America, however, shows the avidity with which new appliances were adopted there. It developed first in the nineteenth century in the commercial context of preserving and transporting meat. By 1920, domestic refrigerators were available in the form of large wood-cased cabinets, often with the coolant mechanism awkwardly protruding. Cheap methods of producing refrigerator bodies were perfected in the 1930s, using processes developed in the automobile industry, and by 1941, sixty per cent of the American population owned a refrigerator.

The method of production heavily conditioned the form. Techniques of pressing and stamping metal were at that time only capable of forming sheet in wide curves and soft radii – features found, for example, in Loewy's 'Coldspot' design, and also noticeable in automobile body designs of the

120 In the Berry 'Magicoal' electric fires of the 1920s technical advance was subordinated to stylistic fantasy

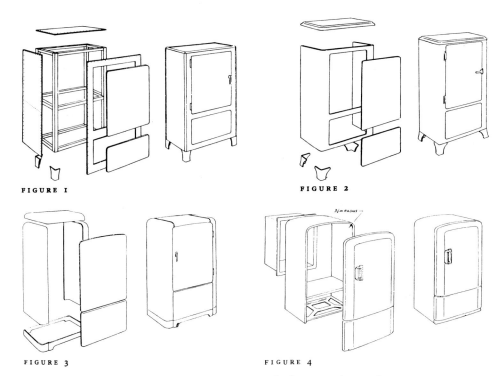

FIGURE 1   FIGURE 2

FIGURE 3   FIGURE 4

121 Harold van Doren's drawings of the evolution of refrigerator design: fig. 1, pre-First World War; fig. 2, 1918–1933; fig. 3, pressed panels as designed by Lurelle Guild for the Norge company, 1933; fig. 4, Westinghouse pressed panels, 1939

period. The relation of refrigerator-form to developments in manufacturing techniques was discussed by Harold van Doren in an article, 'Streamlining: Fad or Function?' in *Design* magazine in 1949. In a series of illustrations he demonstrated the tendency towards reducing the number of component sections, culminating in the technique introduced by the Westinghouse company in 1939 of forming the entire shell from a single sheet of metal in a press known as a 'bulldozer', which eliminated the need for a structural frame. The curved outlines resulting from these production methods, argued Van Doren, were 'imposed on the designer *by the necessity of obtaining low cost through high-speed production*'. The consequences were twofold: refrigerators were reduced in price and became available to a large proportion of the population; but the need to compete by using similar production techniques led to a general similarity of form, with the designer's

121

ingenuity 'taxed to breaking point to produce distinctiveness for his particular client within fixed outlines'. It was not until the 1950s that improvements in methods and materials made sharp edges and pointed corners feasible, but these, too, were universally adopted, and the problem of uniformity was simply transposed to another style.

The pattern of increased volume-production coupled with convergence of form is found across the whole range of consumer products, setting problems for designers and consumers that will be discussed in a later chapter.

A gas or electric cooker, and other implements to which electric heating elements were applied, such as kettles, coffee percolators, toasters and frying pans, made cooking easier, quicker and cleaner. Essentially, however, they did not change the nature of the work, which was the case with a second category of electric appliances, in which motors provided power to perform a task or function. Small electric motors of about one horsepower were fitted to industrial machines by 1900, and in the following decade were adapted to manual appliances, with results that were cumbersome but effective. Gradually, more successfully integrated forms were evolved and new applications were explored.

In the same period prior to the First World War, the first of what became a spate of publications extolling the virtues and benefits of electricity began to appear, such as Maud Lancaster's *Electric Cooking, Heating, Cleaning, etc.*, published in 1914. 'I am convinced', she wrote, 'that [electricity] will be looked upon as one of the greatest blessings in daily life in providing the home with *economic labour- and dirt-saving service.* . . .' From the large number of examples she discussed and illustrated, it is clear that by then, virtually every major category of domestic electrical appliance had achieved a level of efficiency, and often a basic form, that might later be refined, emphasizing aesthetic presentation, but was to remain unaltered in essential principles. General availability required two further stages of development: the provision of electric power around-the-clock, and adaptation to mass-production. In the 1920s work was begun, and by the following decade was well advanced, on the construction of generating grids in the industrial countries and major centres of urban population elsewhere. Small portable generators were also available for use in rural areas.

The main domestic labour-saving applications of electric motors were in cleaning and washing. Innumerable models of manually operated carpet sweepers had been invented by the turn of the century, varying considerably in size and efficiency. One of the most effective was patented in 1876 by Melville R. Bissell, another in the long line of Americans combining inventiveness with great entrepreneurial skill. Many types of sweeper stirred up dust, simply relocating rather than collecting it, but Bissell's design had

150

revolving brushes on a cylinder driven by the wheels, within an enclosed grained-timber case to trap the dust.

This basic principle was combined with electric-powered suction in a machine patented in 1908 by Murray Spangler, whose relative, William Hoover, financed its production and gave the company his name. The format used by Spangler became one of the established types of vacuum cleaner. The Hoover company's early models were effective, but utilitarian *122* in appearance, the motor protruding vertically from the case. By the 1930s, however, the motor became invisible, its presence often marked only by a swelling in the enveloping shroud-designs that became the norm. Dreyfuss' designs for Hoover in 1935 encased the motor in an elliptical housing set *123* above a smoothly curved brush-casing. It was very restrained compared with some competitors' designs that employed dynamically curved biomorphic shapes, often finished in gleaming chrome-plate, drawing freely on the space-ship imagery of contemporary science-fiction films such as the Buck Rogers serials. The element of fantasy in such designs pales when compared to the German 'Silva-fix' model by an unknown designer, the body of which was a large fish in moulded plastic, with appliances plugging into its mouth.

The type of cleaner evolved by Spangler was fundamentally a modification of an existing manual form by new technology. A second basic type applied identical technical principles to the function of cleaning, but owed little to previous models and evolved in a completely different form. Exactly who developed it is not clear, but in 1915 it had been perfected by the Swedish firm of Electrolux as a compact horizontal cylinder with a flexible *124* hose to the cleaning nozzle. Not only carpets, but any surface or material at any height, such as curtain rails and furnishing fabrics, could be cleaned by it. Introduced into the United States in 1924, it was so successful that manufacturers of upright cleaners were forced to develop attachments to perform the same tasks, in order to compete.

Cleaning and dusting by hand were laborious, and the vacuum cleaner was a great time-saver, but the washing machine surely deserves a supreme place of honour in any design pantheon, for relieving the most heavy drudgery in domestic work. Before its advent, those who could afford to sent washing out to laundries or to women who needed to earn extra money. For women with large families, or those for whom it was a livelihood, laundering was a physically exhausting slog.

Once again, America led the way with mass-production of electric spin-washers in the 1930s. In early models the mechanisms were set in an open steel supporting frame; later they were encased in enamelled steel-sheet to assume the box-like form of cookers and refrigerators.

The only THOROUGH Spring Clean

With an ordinary vacuum cleaner you'll take up the loose surface dust —but no more.
Will you stop there? Or will you get rid of the destructive, embedded grit and the dirt that's thickly matted in the carpet's pile?
You must BEAT that out. Only beating will bring it to the surface for air suction to clean it away. And only the Hoover BEATS.
The Hoover beats, sweeps and suc-

tion cleans in one dustless operation while your carpets are still on the floor—makes spring cleaning effort-less and absolutely thorough.
Before you spring clean have a home demonstration of the Hoover, com-plete with the Hoover dusting Tools that clean dustlessly from floor to ceiling. And simultaneously—so that you can judge for yourself—a dem-onstration of the best ordinary vacuum cleaner you know.

A British Empire Product

The HOOVER
REG. TRADE MARK
It BEATS ... as it Sweeps ... as it Cleans

To Prove Carpets Need Beating: Turn over a corner of a carpet; with the handle of an ordinary table knife, or something of equal weight, give the back of the carpet 15 to 25 sharp taps, and watch the dirt dance out from the pile depths on to a piece of paper; feel the destructive character of this grit. This is the dirt your present cleaning methods have missed and that beating has dis-lodged. Correct to the surface the Hoover causes the embedded dirt to be whirled to the surface by the rapid, gentle beating of the Hoover brush, as powerful suction lifts the carpet from the floor and draws all the beaten-out, swept-up dirt into the dust-tight bag.

HOOVER LTD., 229-233 REGENT STREET, LONDON. W.1, and at Birmingham, Manchester, Leicester, Leeds and Glasgow

122–3 Variations in vacuum-cleaner design: (above) Hoover 1926 model with upright motor-housing; (right) Hoover 'Jubilee' model, 1935, with the motor on a horizontal rather than a vertical axis enabling a sleeker, integrated form to be evolved

124 Used on detachable runners or, as shown, with a pistol grip, the Electrolux Model III, first produced in 1915, was light and flexible in use

125–6 Siemens 'Xcel' electric iron of 1926 was one of the earliest to use design as a marketing device. In the General Electric steam- and spray-iron of 1957, the moulded plastic handle has to perform additional functions that influence its form

The final stage of laundering was also transformed, by electric irons, which, being small and relatively inexpensive, were probably the first electric appliances to be almost universally adopted. An AEG catalogue of 1896 included eight models with turned and carved handles in a variety of configurations, including cantilever forms that were subsequently to be revived and marketed as innovations. Most early designs were for use in commercial laundries. The breakthrough into mass-production for domestic use came in 1912, when the American Heater Company of Detroit marketed their low-priced 'American Beauty' model. This was a very neat design for the time, with a smoothly rounded body and lathe-turned wooden handle, and it proved enormously popular.

A defect of early electric irons was their large rear connecting-plug, which made them difficult to stand on end. This problem was resolved by a direct internal connection, with the rear-end and handle combined into a stable base on which the iron could be rested. Technical innovations such as the automatic thermostat and the steam-iron led to further refinements of detail, but the forms established early on remained the basis of development. *125*

The General Electric steam- and spray-iron introduced in 1957 illustrates the general tendency in form and materials. The sole-plate was of cast aluminium, the body encased in chrome-plated steel. The moulded plastic handle had become more substantial in volume than older wooden forms, becoming a focal point for stylistic differentiation. Ergonomically shaped to fit the hand, the forward angle of its front profile was the exact reverse of the casing prow, the overall lines being similarly balanced and integrated. *126*

127 'Revere Ware' designed by W. Archibald Welden and produced from 1939

Changes in social habits have gone hand-in-hand with design developments. A feature of peasant cooking the world over is the limited range of cooking utensils it requires, one large vessel frequently sufficing to produce composite meals. The diversification of diet and culinary methods is a subject in itself, but has been reflected in the specialization of vessels and implements, and their production in a succession of new materials.

Cast iron and tin sheet were widely used in the nineteenth century for pots, pans and baking tins. The development of techniques of coating cast iron with a layer of porcelain enamel gave rise to substantial industry in Germany and Austria by 1850. Enamelware was easier to use and clean than untreated metal, though its colour-range was limited, a deep-blue predominating. Its use declined in the 1920s, though the emerging fashion for gourmet cooking in the 1950s led to a revival of high-quality wares, such as the French Le Creusot range, their solid forms enhanced by a range of bright colours produced by modern chemical processes. Tinware has never been entirely superseded, and continues to be stamped out in diverse forms to produce decorative shapes in cooking and baking.

Aluminium had long been known, but implements in this material were not produced in quantity until around 1910. In 1934 Lurelle Guild designed a successful series of aluminium cooking utensils for the Wear Ever company, specifically adapted to solve the heat-conduction problems of electric cookers and with heat-resistant plastic handles integrated into plain, well-

128 Tupperware polythene bowls as illustrated in a *House Beautiful* article of 1947 to 'honor fine design'. The bowls were described as art objects, with a 'profile as good as a piece of sculpture'

proportioned vessels. Their detailed attention to form and function was an important factor in ensuring the acceptance of unaccustomed materials in such mass-produced wares.

A more dramatic impact could be created by the application of materials such as stainless steel, chrome-plated steel and heat-proof glass, which contributed to an aesthetic emphasis that transformed cooking utensils' utilitarian image. The Revere Copper and Brass Company in America developed a method of plating copper to the base of stainless-steel cooking vessels, giving superior heat distribution. The combination of improved function and the attractive appearance of stainless steel and copper was embodied in a high-quality range marketed in 1939 under the title of 'Revere Ware', designed by W. A. Welden, the company's head of design, in simple *127* but distinctive forms.

Kitchen implements and containers went through a similar evolution, with the difference that plastics were the predominant new materials. Following the patenting of 'Bakelite' by Dr Leo Baekeland in 1907, small items such as egg-cups, sink-strainers and bowls in heat-moulded phenolic plastics became widely available. The introduction of polystyrene in 1938 enabled an even greater range of goods to be produced cheaply. Polystyrene was an important component of synthetic rubber, and production boomed during the war, creating a capacity that was turned to consumer goods after 1945.

An example of the potential of new materials was provided by polyethylene, first produced in 1942. It was flexible but very durable, and was used by a plastics-moulder, Earl C. Tupper, to develop a range of multi-purpose kitchen storage-containers. These were very functional, with a clever airtight lid, and were produced in a variety of forms and translucent colours. In 1947 they were featured in an article by the American magazine *House Beautiful* under the title 'Fine Art for 39 cents'.

Since the Second World War, synthetic plastics have become ever more ubiquitous and dominant, and their types and capacities have been constantly extended. The flexibility possible in their moulding and their wide range of colours has been applied to a bewildering variety of functions, making them one of the most powerful instruments of change in the visual environment.

Not only have homes and workplaces become more hygienic in the twentieth century, but there has been greater emphasis on personal care, reflected in the production of quantities of appliances in diverse forms. Maud Lancaster in 1914 illustrated many items in this category, such as a hair dryer in an inverted L-shaped form that has basically remained unaltered, despite multifarious variations in casings and colours. The male market was broached when the researches of Colonel Jacob Schick produced a tiny but powerful electric motor to drive a shaving-head. The Schick electric razor appeared in 1931, and was sheathed in a smoothly rounded plastic casing, proportioned to fit conveniently into the hand.

The mass-production of domestic consumer products became so widespread in America during the 1930s and 1940s that a full account of design developments during that period would take on encyclopaedic proportions. The transformation they effected in the domestic life of millions was enormous, cumulatively creating an image of a high material standard of living to which most other societies aspired. The extent to which such aspirations were capable of realization, however, was heavily conditioned by variations in economic and social structures and beliefs.

CHAPTER TEN

Play, learning, work and leisure

Design in the modern period is distinguished by an unprecedented degree of diversity and specialization, not only in economic structures and occupational categories, but also in attitudes towards the different phases of individual life. We no longer consider life as a continuum, but as a series of distinct phases, such as childhood, adulthood, old age; and within each phase, sharp divisions of activity have emerged, such as learning and play, work and leisure, with a corresponding opportunity in design to focus on the specific needs of these differentiated groups and activities.

The attitude, for example, that childhood is a distinct phase of life, in which one must be consciously prepared for adulthood and work, is a comparatively recent phenomenon; and indeed, still does not apply to certain levels of society in many parts of the world. Such concepts of play and learning, however, relating to a protected and preparatory phase of childhood have provided a platform for a prolific range of designs, most notably for the toy industry, which has grown into a major area of industrial production.

In its extent and diversity, the history of toys is a microcosm of the evolution of industrial design, with a continuous flow of innovations, new technology and materials constantly being introduced, yet never entirely replacing old forms, so that traditional craft-forms of wooden toys from Eastern Europe and Asia can still be found alongside the most sophisticated electronic playthings.

The origins of the toy industry are difficult to trace in detail, but in the nineteenth century two important strands of development emerged. In Germany, a well-established cottage industry gradually coalesced into larger workshops that finally became factory-based industries, by 1900 establishing a large international trade and export market. In America, in contrast, toys began to be produced in New England by mid-century applying techniques of mechanization and mass-production similar to those used in other industries. Tin-plate, cast iron and ingenious clockwork mechanisms and devices were extensively and often imaginatively utilized.

By the early twentieth century, toy industries were well established in many countries. The range of products they manufactured was staggering, but at the risk of over-simplifying such a plethora of forms, two broad categories can be discerned. The first type of toy is a miniature version of the contemporary adult world, providing opportunities for imaginative role-playing, such as dolls and cooking stoves, soldiers and train sets. The second type is intended to provide children with opportunities for imaginative exploration of a more free-ranging kind; the toys may allow role-playing, but are not specifically designed for this purpose. An important innovator in this field was a German architect, Dr Ernst Froebel. The 'Kindergartens' he established, and the theories based on his experience, profoundly influenced child-education, balancing concepts of the need for a social context as essential for the development of infants, with a belief in learning through exploratory activities. To this latter end he designed many toys, including the Froebel blocks, a range of geometric wooden forms capable of being assembled in endless variations. They were subsequently made famous by their influence on Frank Lloyd Wright, who claimed to derive many of his architectural and design theories from a set provided by his mother, a committed disciple of Froebel.

A modern variant of this type is the 'Lego' system, developed in embryo by a Danish toy-maker, Ole Kirk Christiansen, in the late 1930s, and further evolved after the war by his son Godtfred into a modular system of coloured, plastic, interlocking bricks. The simplicity of the component units allows total flexibility in use, providing a classic example of the creative possibilities of modular systems.

The products of Frank Hornby encompassed both categories. The model train systems bearing his name, first clockwork and later powered by electric motors, became household names in Britain, as did a range of die-cast model vehicles marketed under the title 'Dinky' toys. In 1901, however, Hornby patented a model-engineering constructional system, later to be known as 'Meccano', which comprised standard components such as metal ribs, struts and plates, fastened by nuts and bolts. This was capable of adaptation to a wide range of ages and abilities, enabling models of both elemental simplicity, and, with the application of gears and motors, great mechanical complexity, to be built.

In many countries the late nineteenth century was a period of considerable expansion in educational provision, institutionalizing the concept of childhood, and stimulating a number of industries that supplied furniture, fittings and implements for teaching purposes. School desks emerged very clearly as a specific type, with a combined writing-surface and bench-seat of timber supported on a cast-iron frame. The attached seats and serried ranks in which they were arranged reflected the didactic formality of teaching methods. More informal methods in the twentieth century resulted in

129

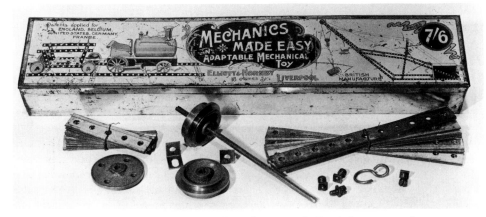

129 Frank Hornby's original 1901 tin box of 'Mechanics Made Easy', forerunner of the Meccano system

designs for furniture capable of being flexibly grouped, and ergonomic studies have alleviated the worst discomforts of the older forms.

The growth of education and its expanding material needs created considerable commercial opportunities, leading many companies to commission designers for new forms and ideas. By the early 1950s, some fifty million dollars was being spent annually on school furniture in the United States, a figure that influenced the Brunswick Corporation, specialists in sports equipment, to diversify into this field, in 1952 engaging Dave Chapman to design a complete system of school furniture for them. In designing for a firm new to the demands of educational use, he was able to work unhampered by habit and convention, evolving a unit system using plain timber surfaces and tubular steel for supports, intended to provide all the requirements of a classroom. The forms were strong and elemental, relying on the warm tones and grain of the timber for colour and pattern. The elements could be variably arranged to suit different teaching programmes and the space available.

Although mass-production and improved design have influenced the physical context of education, teaching, at all levels, has so far remained little affected by mechanization and technological progress. Its stage of development is analogous to the early phases of industrialization, with expanded needs being met by a multiplication of traditional methods in larger institutions. A limited use of mechanical aids has been pioneered in instructional programmes developed for the armed forces and businesses, as with the overhead projector that allows texts and diagrams written or drawn on clear acetate sheets to be projected by an illuminated platten. Introduced

159

in the 1950s, it has made some inroads on the use of blackboards and chalk. The projection of visual material has also been stimulated by efficient automatic slide-projectors, such as the Kodak Carousel, designed in Germany by Hans Gugelot and first introduced in 1961. The basis of his design was the interaction of geometric elements. Instead of a lateral slide-change from an open tray, he employed a vertical change from an enclosed circular tray positioned on top of a rectangular projector which provided a stable base. The mechanism could be operated by a small hand-held remote-control unit. A sophisticated range of interchangeable lenses and accessories gave the projector a diverse range of application on a standardized body.

The most systematic technological transformation has been the introduction of language laboratories, consisting of individual carrels equipped with headphones and controls, linked to a central tape-recorder console, enabling students to respond simultaneously, but individually, to teaching sequences. Such innovations, however, have only supplemented traditional methods.

Some efforts have been made to explore the possibilities of new technology applied to education. In the late 1960s, the Dutch electrical company, Philips, produced a speculative design for a learning unit. This had an air of science-fiction fantasy when compared to the reality of most classrooms. A large integrated console in white moulded plastic was equipped with video and audio equipment, giving access to a wide range of information-sources. The cost of such units was a major obstacle to their adoption, but Philips demonstrated that radical revision of the tools of learning was feasible. The Open University, commencing in 1969 in Britain, was a more practical venture, using a combination of public media, television and radio, and publications and kits, for home-based study programmes. The basic concept was not new, but the range of means applied were. In 1972, for example, a mass-produced microscope designed by Dr

130 The Kodak Carousel slide-projector designed by Hans Gugelot, 1961

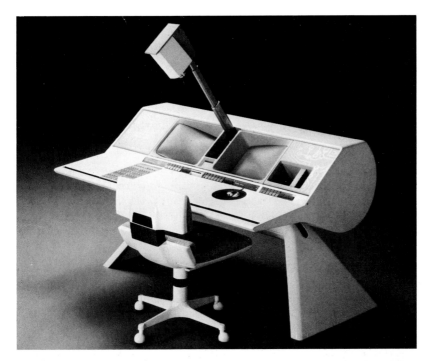

131 Philips' experimental design project TELL (Teacher-aiding Electronic Learning Link), designed under Knut Yran and first presented in 1970

132 The Open University microscope of 1972 designed by Dr John MacArthur. Measuring only 5 × 3 × 1 in., it was inexpensive and highly versatile

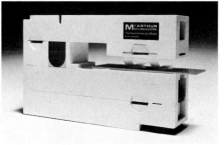

John MacArthur was introduced. Produced in white moulded plastic, it was *132* lightweight and inexpensive, adaptable to variable light sources and capable of use in the field. It made this instrument generally accessible for the first time. Its modest scale was in direct contrast to the Philips console, but the approach to design it embodies has enormous potential, in facilitating an education available throughout life, and adaptable to both individual needs and changing social circumstances.

In contrast with education, work-processes have changed profoundly during the last two centuries. If personal choice has been widened in creating the home environment, the situation is very different for people working outside the home, whose conditions often have little relationship to them as individuals, emphasizing instead their role as functionaries in industrial, commercial or governmental structures. In the choice of equipment and fittings for factories and offices, employees are rarely consulted.

An exception was the Osram Company in Germany, producing lighting and electrical equipment, which in 1927 established a planning committee with a brief to take account of workers' welfare as well as organizational and technical questions, with a view to increased productivity. A network of twenty sub-committees included representatives from all parts of the firm, with a brief to consider beauty as well as function in the reorganization of workplaces. Comfortable standard furniture, bright, warm colours, functional lighting, noise reduction and better ventilation were introduced, with improved changing- and dining-rooms, and roof-gardens for refreshment and recreation.

Transport vehicles and systems have provided some of the most far-reaching examples of changes in the working environment. Here, emphasis is no longer solely on external forms, but also includes consideration of human physical and psychological reactions in relation to performance and safety. In the nineteenth century, for example, the cabs of steam locomotives were laid out in a cluttered pattern derived from the mechanical structure, that made no concessions to the operatives. Even in the twentieth century, *133* driver and fireman still had to adapt to the machine, which required a considerable degree of physical dexterity and acquired skill. Modern cab-layouts on diesel and electric locomotives, in contrast, have been influenced by improvements in the design of aircraft cockpits, stemming from the Second World War, when the need for split-second reactions in fighter-plane combat stimulated ergonomic studies to co-ordinate controls and instruments. The influence of aircraft design is evident in the cab of the *134* 'bullet trains' designed by a research team of Japan National Railways for the high-speed Tokkaido line from 1963 onwards. With padded seats, simplified, accessible controls and clear forward vision, they represented a new image of train-operation.

The significance of the nature of the work-process, however, as distinct from the physical conditions in which it is performed, was demonstrated in the 1960s by the reactions of drivers in Britain who were transferred from dirty and arduous jobs on steam trains to diesel or electric locomotives. Many experienced difficulty, finding the cabs and controls of the new vehicles too simple, that is, making few demands on their intelligence and skills, and therefore less satisfying to operate.

Buses and heavy goods vehicles have also undergone radical change. The considerable physical effort of driving such vehicles, and the fatiguing effects

162

133 Driver and fireman at work on the *Flying Scotsman* locomotive of the London and North Eastern Railway. Photographed by James Jarché in 1932

134 Driver's cab of 'Type 962' experimental trains constructed by Hitachi for service on the Tokkaido line of Japan National Railways

of noise and vibration, have been mitigated, with simplified power-assisted controls, comfortable seating, better suspension and insulation contributing to an improvement in driving conditions. On grounds of both efficiency and safety, the vastly increased size and operational range of the heavy goods vehicles of the 1960s necessitated a sweeping reappraisal of the relationship between driver and machine. The DAF 'F2600' heavy truck of 1964, manufactured in Holland, embodied many important improvements, the most immediately evident being the larger cab, its impression of spaciousness enhanced by the light colours used on internal roof- and wall-panelling. New standards of comfort were epitomized by individual seats of a form previously associated with executive suites. Designed to provide a relaxed operating posture, they were wide, well upholstered and had broad arm-rests. The controls and instruments were formed and grouped for instant recognition and ease of operation, and window-pattern afforded clear all-round vision. Heavy insulation reduced noise-levels, and there was an efficient heating and ventilation system. Two bunks at the rear provided for rests on long journeys.

Despite a convergence of visual forms and design concepts, the nature of work on road-vehicles is markedly different from that on trains and aircraft, still demanding continuous control and personal judgment that have not been reduced by external aids such as automatic train-control and automatic pilots and landing-aids for aircraft. The trend to automation increases safety, however, and future developments in road transport may follow the same direction.

Paradoxically, while improvements in the design of heavy road-vehicles recognize the importance of human physical and psychological well-being, the huge vehicles themselves pose an increasingly serious environmental threat.

It is in offices and factories that the inability of increasingly mechanized and automated work-processes to provide satisfaction or fulfilment for the workers who operate them is most acute. In this context, there are limits to the improvements designers can achieve. The performance of tasks can be made easier and safer, but no improvements in design can make a boring job satisfying or alter its basic nature. This depends far more on changes in social and economic attitudes and organization.

One of the most widespread reactions to the stresses of industrial work has been pressure for shorter working hours and increased holidays, resulting, in most industrialized countries, in a general increase of free time and an extension of the concept of leisure. Parallel to this tendency has been a considerable expansion of designs for leisure activities. In the field of entertainment, technological innovation and mass-production have brought a change of emphasis from public and communal forms, such as theatres, music-halls and sporting events, at which spectators are participants by their presence, to home-based forms such as radio and television.

When broadcasting began in the 1920s, the component units of radios – receiver, tuner and loudspeaker – became available as separate parts, often in kits requiring an element of technical participation from the user. The extension of broadcasting and extensive technical refinements completely changed this concept. By 1930, manufacturers in many countries had begun to emphasize that a radio should be a piece of furniture, capable of being accepted in the home. As a result, the component units were grouped in a unified casing, with simple controls for volume, tone and tuning. The progression can be seen in a sequence of designs over a period of ten years for the German company, Telefunken. The 'Alpha' set of 1927 had the *135* appearance of a technical appliance with little attempt at refinement. It was dominated by the large valves protruding from a plain box of natural wood, and required a separate loudspeaker extension. The 'Wiking 125 WL' of 1933 *136* marks the transition to unified models with a case of moulded bakelite styled in stepped Art Deco fashion. A built-in loudspeaker placed above the concealed receiver and tuning-units gave a pronounced vertical emphasis. The appearance of the 'T644W' set of 1936–7, with a walnut-veneered *137* casing, is the culmination of the radio-as-furniture concept, accentuating external qualities of form and materials. The positioning of the loudspeaker alongside other units gave a low profile, enabling horizontal lines to be stressed.

With transistors replacing bulky valves and circuitry in the 1950s, large radios were gradually replaced by small portable instruments, generally in a plastic housing. In 1957 Sony of Japan produced an all-transistor radio, the 'Type 63', epitomizing this trend towards reduction in scale. The level of *138* technical innovation was hardly reflected in its external design, however, which consisted of a coloured plastic casing, to which an anodized metal-gauze loudspeaker was riveted, with a relatively large tuning control protruding. Later models were revised to give a crisply delineated rectangular form with recessed controls.

The gramophone has also undergone many formal and technical changes, from the early wind-up spring-powered sets with a large acoustic horn, replaced in the 1930s by electrically powered units with a built-in loudspeaker that were presented, like radios, as heavily styled pieces of furniture, to the recent small and very sophisticated pieces of electronic engineering, offered with the matching units of modern high-fidelity equipment, their form emphasizing technical innovation with a plethora of controls and dials. They have been joined by tape-recorders, especially since

135–7 Three radios by Telefunken showing the progression of radio-housing design within a decade: (above) 'Alpha', 1927 and 'Wiking 125 WL', 1933; (left) 'T644W', 1936–7

the tape-cassette initially developed by Philips of Eindhoven in the late 1950s was adopted as an international standard format.

Television became widely available only after the Second World War. Initially, the screens were very small, often only nine inches in width, set in a large unwieldy body, also styled as furniture and frequently clad in timber veneers. In the 1950s technical refinement, particularly the reduced bulk facilitated by transistors, changed the proportions, a larger screen in a more compact body leaving little leeway for designers' stylistic flights. A further change of emphasis came with the introduction of portable battery-powered models, heralding a return to smaller screens. Here, too, Sony led the way *139* with a tiny 'Micro' TV set that had a five-inch screen. Introduced in 1962, it had a simple technical precision which became the dominant theme of the company's approach to design.

Electronic media in the home have become commonplace, and there may be potential harm in the receptivity divorced from immediate personal

139 Sony 'Micro' TV–5–303, 1963, with five-inch screen

138 Sony 'Type 63' transistor radio, 1957, the
first 'shirt pocket' radio

experience that is inherent in their use. It would, nevertheless, be totally
misleading to convey the image of a supine populace being passively
manipulated in their leisure time by such means. Other categories of leisure
activity that have also expanded enormously in the twentieth century are
hobbies, sports and outdoor recreation, based on a high degree of active
participation. As recognition of the market potential of such activities
developed, greater attention to presentation and appearance became
obvious. Household construction and repairs, requiring tools, fixtures and
fittings, have been one such area of growth.

The small electric motor which transformed household work has also
been a vital factor in the growth of the do-it-yourself movement. During the
1920s and 1930s it was applied to heavy duty industrial tools such as drills,

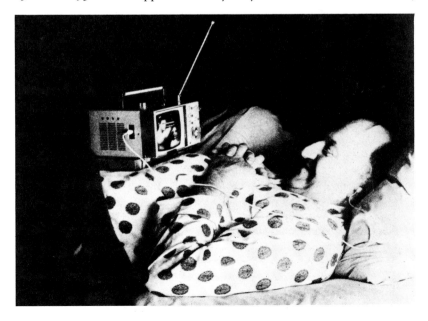

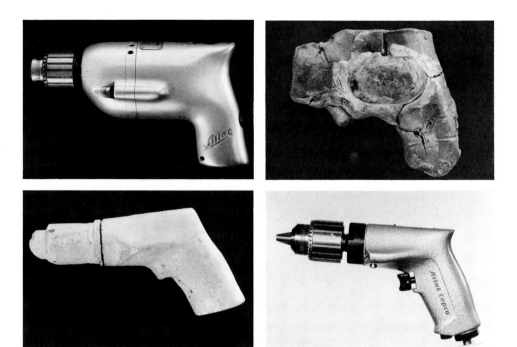

140–3 When Atlas Copco's RAB 300 air-drill of 1948 was found to be uncomfortable and noisy in use, Rune Zernell used ergonomic models and studies by Professor Fritiof Sjostrand to develop an 'eight-hour grip'. This was built around noise-reduction chambers in the redesigned LBB 33 model of 1955

saws, planers and sanders, but after 1945 became available in a wide range of lightweight models, at low prices, opening up new possibilities for the home craftsman. Immediately after the war, for example, the American company Black and Decker marketed an electric drill specifically designed for home use at just under seventeen dollars. Its casing was in a form identified by Reyner Banham as stemming from contemporary science-fiction space-gun imagery, an influence on styling also reflected in designs for American cars of that period – in both cases accompanied by deficiencies in handling and use. Sculptural moulding was not necessarily non-functional, however. A similar

140–3 drill designed in Sweden by Rune Zernell for Atlas Copco in the early 1950s was based on detailed studies of the grip and pressure points of the hand, and these, rather than an imposed stylistic device, determined the form.

Many hand-tools such as screwdrivers and chisels have been redesigned to make use of modern materials. Their handles and grips, in particular, have

168

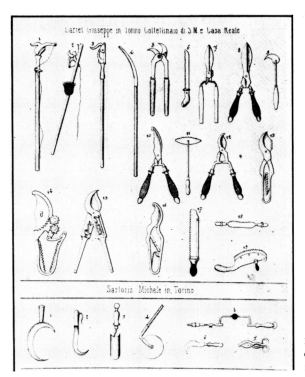

144 Garden tools illustrated in the catalogue of the Turin Exposition, 1858

145 Hulme Chadwick's 'Swoe', first produced in 1958 by Wilkinson Sword

undergone considerable changes in form. Traditionally they were of wood, and turned on a lathe, resulting in rounded continuous curves. The introduction of moulded plastics has enabled new forms based on ergonomic studies to be devised to fit the hand more comfortably and securely.

Gardening was traditionally a means for many people to supplement inadequate food supplies, and indeed frequently remains so, but the growth of prosperity in industrialized countries has transformed it into one of the most popular and satisfying of leisure activities. Many time-honoured

144 implements are still used: a catalogue of the Turin Exposition of 1858 illustrates a range of secateurs, shears, pruning-saws and knives in forms that still abound. Many mechanical devices derived from commercial horticulture have been introduced, however, such as motorized lawn-mowers and rotary-hoes. In addition, traditional tools have frequently been extensively modified or redefined, and in this respect the British firm of Wilkinson Sword has been consistently innovatory. Hulme Chadwick's

145 design for the 'Swoe' of 1958 was a perceptive redefinition of the weeding-hoe which extended its potential in use by allowing, not only a forward and backward action, but also lateral movement to hoe between plants. Produced in stainless steel and with a plastic-coated handle, it was later redesigned in a flowing, integrated form, adding eye-catching appeal to its functional qualities in response to commercial competition in this sector of the market.

Outside the home, design for sporting and recreational pastimes has shown a similar expansion. Many traditionally exclusive sports, such as skiing and golf, have been popularized, and their equipment has been intensively developed and improved.

The growth of motorization has introduced a considerable degree of freedom in outdoor recreations, evident in the multitudinous designs of caravans and trailers, which have not been immune from stylistic influences. Many early models in Europe tended to reveal the influence of horse-drawn gypsy caravans, and there was a period of considerable uncertainty in the

146 forms adopted. The Eccles 'Liberty Hall' caravan of 1934 with curved end roof-lines, bay window and leaded panes echoed the nostalgia for the past found in much of contemporary British design. In contrast, the 'Airstream',

147 produced in the United States to match the Chrysler 'Airflow', vehemently asserted its modernity, its gleaming organic form becoming a cult object. Since the Second World War, vehicles of this type have tended to become a compromise between external forms rounded in profile at each end to reduce wind resistance when towing, and a maximum functional disposal of internal space. The use of aluminium, in particular, and flexible convertible furniture and storage-space have made modern designs lightweight,

146–7 Eccles 'Liberty Hall' caravan, 1934, an example of contemporary nostalgia on wheels, lacking only a thatched roof. In contrast, the 'Airstream' trailer was uncompromisingly modern and became a cult object. The illustration is of a painting by Ralph Goings from 1970.

compact and easy to tow. In general, however, their external appearance is very bland, though the gypsy people who continue to customize their modern vehicles maintain an element of their old traditions of resplendent decoration.

Aluminium tubing and synthetic fabrics have also combined to make camping equipment more portable and colourful, whilst still durable and weather resistant. Accessories and fittings for these activities have also proliferated, freeing them from the old image of hair-shirted rigour and spartan discomfort.

Increased car ownership and the resultant road congestion led many people to take to the water for leisure activities. In 1959 boat ownership in America had reached seven million, the proportions of the boom indicated by an increase of one million in the previous two years. Materials such as aluminium and fibreglass mouldings were used to produce lightweight, impact-resistant hulls that did not rot or warp, and plywood, strengthened by synthetic resin bonding, also made a revival. Sixty per cent were outboard-motor powered, an area dominated in America by the Outboard Marine Corporation, which had two divisions, Evinrude and Johnson Motors. Each produced a motor identical in components and performance, but distinguished by shroud design and graphics, with Brooks Stevens of Milwaukee designing for Evinrude and Dave Chapman for Johnson. The role of design for OMC therefore concentrated on product differentiation. 'Competition sells', stated its President, even if it was self-generated.

The process of popularizing amateur photography for creative and recreational purposes begun by George Eastman in the nineteenth century continued to develop, with cameras becoming more compact and easier to
148 operate. A key-object in the trend towards miniaturization was the Minox camera, designed by Walter Zapp and produced in 1937 by the VEF company in Latvia; a tiny apparatus that was precision-built and highly efficient. Its format was later to be imitated in innumerable cheap pocket cameras in moulded plastic that used cassette-film loading to simplify their use. The post-war period also saw a great expansion in the production of cine-cameras for the popular market, with apparatus becoming smaller and more portable while often incorporating very sophisticated technical improvements, such as automatic light meters and zoom attachments. The
149 8 mm 'Cine Canonet' of 1962 by the Canon company's design team under Hiroshi Shinihara typified the high-quality products that established Japanese dominance in this field from the 1950s onwards, combining numerous innovations within a form having a simple clarity derived from close attention to user-needs.

Motor-cycle design also adapted to increasing use for leisure and sporting

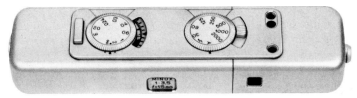

148 The Minox LX, a refinement of the original 1935 model, though the basic form remains unaltered

149 Canon 8 mm 'Cine Canonet' designed by Hiroshi Shinihara, 1962

activities. In this field, too, the impact of Japanese designs from the 1950s onwards was dramatic, destroying British and Italian dominance within a decade, on a foundation of intensive technical research and improvement, high-quality standards in production, and attractive form. The rapidly developing awareness of the importance of appearance in Japanese products is visible in a comparison of the 125 c.c. Kawasaki 'B8' of 1962, squat and heavy in appearance, with the 120 c.c. 'C2TR' of 1967. In the second, the upper lines of tank, seat and carrier are unified, and the exhaust is given a dynamic upward sweep, with an overall combination of polished metal parts

150
151

173

and a range of bright colours creating a dazzling effect. Set against the B8, it had become a 'fun' product.

The examples of designs discussed in this chapter can only be of an indicative nature when set against the bewildering proliferation of industrial products for an ever-wider and ever-more-specialized range of purposes. Since designs are produced for use and application, the context for which they are intended and in which they are used has to be considered in order to understand and evaluate them. The context may be facilitative or determinative in intention or practice, either enabling people to do what they want, at their own pace, or requiring them to achieve predetermined ends within time limits. The aesthetic effect of designs will be largely conditioned by the role and attitudes of users in relation to them.

This clearly creates problems in evaluation, since not only is one faced with a proliferation of forms, but with a variable reaction to them, and it requires that designs be considered in terms of an interaction between their innate qualities, as determined by their designers, and the specific conditions of their application.

Many designers and critics, as described in Chapter Five, have reacted against the multiformity of, and conditional response to design, by attempting to propound a unified aesthetic that has universal validity irrespective of the conditions of use. Yet even when an object is simple and monofunctional, perception of it may vary considerably. Le Corbusier, for example, ended his book *Towards a New Architecture* with an illustration of a

150–1 Motor-cycles are among the most fantastic forms produced by modern industry, though this characteristic is frequently overlooked due to their ubiquity and familiarity: (left, below) 125 c.c. Kawasaki 'B8', 1962; (above) 120 c.c. Kawasaki 'C2TR', 1967

briar pipe that exemplified his idealist, functional aesthetic. In use, however, its value is less rarefied and abstract. To a smoker it can signify personal pleasure and solace; whereas in advertisements, a pipe is frequently used as a symbol of masculinity. To a non-smoker, on the other hand, it may be an offensive portable incinerator for the production of carcinogenous fumes.

Although designers may therefore devise forms with defined purposes and effects in mind, the perception of those forms, and the functional or symbolic values attributed to them by users and observers, will be conditional, influenced by attitudes to the purposes for which products are applied, and the framework in which they are used. This shift of emphasis from the level of abstract, enclosed values to a relative interpretation, does not diminish the aesthetic worth of designed objects, but it does place their evaluation firmly in the complex and variegated context of everyday human experience.

CHAPTER ELEVEN

Mass-production and individual choice

From the viewpoint of designers and the organizations employing them, design is seen in terms of the forms of individual items or a linked range of products. From the standpoint of consumers, on the other hand, it is seen, not in terms of the work of one designer or the products of one company, but as a broad spectrum of types of product of comparable function and price, offering the possibility of choice within each category.

The potential scope for the exercise of choice by consumers has been significantly enlarged by two interrelated developments: first, the provision of an increased volume of products to serve an ever-greater variety of purposes, outlined in the previous chapters; and second, the general expansion of wealth that has enabled more people to purchase these goods.

Mass-production in America was based on acceptance of the right of the greatest possible number to have its products. Economic self-interest was certainly a predominant motive, but was often mixed with a democratic idealism that, although sometimes idiosyncratic, should not be under-estimated. The effect of this essentially American characteristic, but not its origin in social values, was noted in a report on household appliance production in Britain, prepared in 1945 by the research organization Political and Economic Planning, which commented: 'If attention is given to an appliance which is in large-scale demand in the USA, but in low demand in this country, it is found that in the USA, it is commonly bought by much lower income groups than in this country. The adoption of mass-production techniques in the United States in order to market a viable product at a low price therefore reflects a basically different economic attitude that one can find repeated in almost every major area of industrial production.' This was contrasted with the common British practice of concentrating on more expensive appliances for higher income groups. The position in the rest of Europe was similar.

Domestic appliances had at first been seen primarily as a solution to the 'servant problem'. Widening employment opportunities, especially for women, and greater mobility, meant that after the First World War, few people were willing to work in service. The design and production of appliances were therefore stimulated by the need to ease the work-load of middle-class women who, instead of organizing the work of servants, were

152–3 Whether organic or geometric, formal considerations rather than mechanical function dominate the design of electrical goods, as in two models from the same firm in the mid-1970s: (left) 'Polivalente' centrifugal fan by Mario Zanuso; (right) a company design, the 'Vort-Mec' wall-fan, both for Vortice Elettrosociale

faced with the necessity of doing it themselves. The tensions caused by this decline in status and role created a growth-point for the later development of 'Women's Liberation', and it is hardly surprising that domestic appliances feature large in their demonology as a symbol of bondage. For women in lower income groups the power to acquire these same appliances generally came later, from the 1950s onwards, and merely alleviated work they had always had to do.

Following the widespread development of mass-production, purely visual aspects of design came to predominate as the means of attracting the consumer. This emphasis was facilitated by the miniaturization of working parts to the extent that they became structurally insignificant, undermining *152–3* the argument that utilitarian form should reflect mechanical function, and throwing the form taken by the casing or envelope open to expressive possibilities – a tendency powerfully reinforced by the aesthetic potential of new materials, and the augmented range of colours and finishes produced by chemical and metallurgical research.

The vast quantity of machines and appliances that poured out did indeed create a diversity of choice, but the fact that their functional qualities could not be easily perceived made selection fraught with difficulty. This in part explains the reluctance of consumers, even in America, to accept any design that looked radically different. Designers therefore had to strive for a delicate balance between innovation in order to create interest, and reassuringly identifiable elements. Raymond Loewy formulated this approach in his MAYA (most advanced yet acceptable) principle, while Dreyfuss included an element in designs that he called 'survival form'. 'By embodying a familiar pattern in an otherwise wholly new and radical form,' he wrote, 'we can make the unusual acceptable to many people who would otherwise reject it.' Resistance to radical innovation affected not only domestic products, but also technical designs oriented to the volatile nature of consumer preference. The Ariel 'Leader' motor-cycle, for instance, produced in Britain in 1957, had a petrol tank located on the rear frame, but retained a dummy-tank of conventional form. This same device was later repeated on the Japanese Honda 'Gold Wing 1000', the dummy-tank opening in half to reveal electrical controls. In both cases, producers felt unable to present a visual choice to the consumers in face of the power of the conventional image of a motor-cycle, even though its form had become functionally redundant.

There was danger for producers in the time-lag between the preparation of a design and its marketing. Design for mass-production was not a response to public demand, but rather a gamble, attempting to anticipate it. The annual model-change was a marketing device, but also provided a safety-margin for designers, by allowing them to introduce changes gradually and to hedge their bets against miscalculation. The end-result, however, was that as competing companies sought maximum sales and eschewed radical innovation, products in particular categories tended to become more and more homogeneous.

In the 1950s, American automobiles, for instance, became very similar to one another, and in this case too, there was little reference to function, the manufacturers collectively embarking on essays in pure style, to which consumers enthusiastically responded. Attempts to introduce more operationally economic and simple forms, on European lines, such as Loewy's designs for Studebaker, and small cars such as the Nash 'Metropolitan', met with little success as American cars competed to become bigger, more powerful, grandiose and colourful. The Cadillac Coupé of 1948, designed by a General Motors styling team under Harley Earl, was the first to sprout tail-fins, which became the most controversial design feature of this phase, and by 1955, in the Cadillac 'Eldorado', they had grown to maturity. The fins were only part of the trend, however, the whole design being a jet-age image of speed, the hood sleekly sweeping back from the bonnet, and the tail fanning out from the low-slung body to end with the blast from sculptured jet exhausts. The functional deficiencies of these fuel-greedy behemoths were notorious, but to discuss them in such terms would be to miss the point. They were an image of the wealth and power that

154 General Motors Cadillac 'Eldorado' Brougham, 1955, advertised as 'styled in the mode of jet aircraft'. A critic commented on this style: 'Never has it been so hard to see the basic substance of a car'

suddenly became, or seemed to become, accessible to Americans in the postwar boom, with the realms of fantasy democratized and available to all.

The end of the dream, and the reassertion of a sense of social reality came with economic recession in 1958, precisely the point at which Ford, riding the wave of the previous years, produced the 'Edsel', a summary of the stylistic trends of the mid-1950s, at a development cost of $250 million, and made staggering losses. The other automobile companies were also hard hit, since they had all concentrated on the same type of product in the same general style. With recession, and a turning away from big, expensive vehicles, smaller cars imported from Europe, and later Japan, offering different concepts of form and function, began to make ever-deeper inroads on the market.

Although the wave of exoticism in 1950s' American automobile design passed, it revealed fundamental problems that in greater or lesser degree have become increasingly evident in consumer societies. The design of products is directed to consumers' conscious and unconscious aspirations, as much as to suggest actual benefits or functions. Concepts of a desired way of life have come to be defined in material terms, with the appropriate products regarded as necessities. Such items could, if desired, be used to create a fantasy world, but this world was revealed as transient and unstable, with the current dream rendered obsolete by next year's model. As mass-production became concentrated in a small number of large companies, the quantitative increase in production was necessarily accompanied, and indeed was only

157

155–6 Convergence of form is apparent in two competing Italian washing machines of the mid-1970s: (left) Sangiorgio 'Tema 164' and (right) Zerowatt '955'

155–6 made possible, by a reduction in size of the ranges of goods produced, and at the same time, the designs of competitive models converged. The reduction in number of true options, combined with the pressure on consumers to buy repeatedly, led the American designer Don Wallance to refer to 'the misery of choice'.

A widespread response has been the establishment of consumer organizations, such as Consumers' Union in America, founded in 1935, which led the way in developing techniques of comparative testing of products. Ralph Nader, a member of the Board of Consumers' Union, established a new pattern of consumer militancy in 1965 with his book *Unsafe at any Speed*, a swingeing attack on the American automobile industry. The pressure from such organizations has had beneficial results, mainly in legislation to protect consumers on such matters as safety and guarantees. Their tests and comparisons are based on rational analyses of function and performance. Yet consumer choice is rarely an exercise in logic, and the value of forms, often instinctively perceived, remains a decisive factor in determining preferences. The lack of correlation between attractive form and desired function remains an unsolved dilemma.

157 Although the modular units were originally derived from concepts of efficient work patterns, modern kitchen design increasingly emphasizes the owner's lifestyle and status, representing a world of fantasy rather than work

CHAPTER TWELVE

Design and politics

If personal choice in relation to consumer products has been diminished in many respects, it has become minimal in those aspects of design subject to government influence, while, at the same time, the scope of indirect and direct bureaucratic influence has been continually expanded. The subordination of design to political ends makes the need to consider the context in which designs are produced and used nowhere more relevant than in the realm of government intervention.

The stresses of industrialization created social problems of a dimension and magnitude beyond solution by individuals and voluntary groups, no matter how great their concern. A considerable increase in governmental power therefore became necessary in the nineteenth century, at both central and local levels, in order to direct and regulate to mitigate the worst excesses of misery and disease in overcrowded cities. The scale of developments such as the expansion of the railway networks similarly required government intervention in a regulatory role. Although the influence of state regulation on railway design, for instance, was largely indirect, as with the definition of safety regulations, it could sometimes have fundamental consequences. After a Parliamentary inquiry in 1845–6, the 4 foot $8\frac{1}{2}$ inch track-gauge was defined as standard in Britain, ending attempts by Isambard Kingdom Brunel and the Great Western Railway to establish the 7 foot gauge. The latter had many advantages, allowing larger engines capable of faster speeds, more spacious passenger accommodation and a more stable and comfortable ride, but the overwhelming preponderance of narrow-gauge mileage and its numerous supporters in Parliament brought an inevitable victory, and henceforward designers had to work within its constraints. Modern legislation on standards and safety has often had a similar conditioning effect in establishing a framework for designs.

A further indirect influence stems from the growth of bureaucracies in official or semi-official bodies. The increased size and scope of government in modern societies, whatever their position in the ideological spectrum, has meant the establishment of administrative means enabling them to exercise their augmented power. The procurement of equipment by government agencies has correspondingly grown to an extent that often determines the fortunes of products. An order for items such as typewriters or vehicles in large quantities could provide a valuable platform for mass-production.

The scale of requirements has also generated specific designs for government purposes, with bodies such as the Ministry of Works in Britain and the US Federal Supply Service establishing design departments in the 1950s. Their range of work for government offices and military and diplomatic establishments was often very extensive, but their designs were generally conservative, stressing functional acceptability to the user. A feature of such designs is the image they frequently provide of hierarchical organization, as with furniture indicating progression in rank or grade by such means as increments in the surface area of desks, type and size of chairs, and variations of materials, colour and finish.

Many governments also came to recognize that economic success depended, not only on material and cost factors, but also on qualities of workmanship and appearance, resulting in initiatives to provide a flow of trained designers for industry. The lead in this respect was taken by France, where by the late eighteenth century, a network of schools teaching design was established in the major cities. In 1771, in Paris alone, some fifteen hundred students were being specifically trained to work in industry, and in the following century, the 'Ecoles des Arts et Métiers' continued to provide a cadre of skilled pattern-designers who were largely responsible for establishing the reputation of French design in matters of artistic taste.

It became clear in Britain by the 1830s that technical and economic advantages, though considerable, were insufficient to secure commercial predominance. In a speech in the House of Commons in 1832, Sir Robert Peel declared: 'It is well known that our manufacturers were, in all matters connected with machinery, superior to all their foreign competitors; but in pictorial designs, which were so important in recommending the production of industry to the taste of the consumer, they were unfortunately, not equally successful; and hence they had found themselves unequal to cope with their rivals.' Concern was sufficiently widespread for a Select Committee to be established by Parliament, to 'inquire into the best means of extending a knowledge of the arts and of the principles of design among the people (especially the manufacturing population) of the country . . .'. The evidence submitted indicated a clear lack of trained designers, with a costly tendency to import foreign designs. The Select Committee attributed this to inadequate educational facilities for artists and artisans, and recommended the establishment of schools of design on the French model. Subsequent attempts to implement this proposal were hampered, however, by extended and often acrimonious debates over the relevance of academic art-training to the needs of industry, a problem that remained unresolved in

Britain for over a century. Although the government could make policy decisions and establish schools, it was incapable of changing social and aesthetic attitudes that made the realization of its policies impossible.

In other countries, however, social prejudice against industry was less influential, and by the early twentieth century, Austria, Germany, Sweden and Switzerland, among others, had state-supported systems of art education, which extended concepts of design beyond pattern-making, taking into consideration materials, structures and the nature of design-problems. High-level technical and engineering education was also a notable source of talent in industrial design.

After the Second World War, legislation was enacted in many countries establishing patterns of design education specifically oriented to the needs of industry, in most cases justified by the importance of design in increasingly competitive export markets vital to sustain national income.

This same justification provided the rationale for promotional exhibitions and displays of industrial goods organized by government agencies – events which not only provided employment for designers, but frequently featured innovations that profoundly influenced forms and fashions in design. Again, France led the way. Following the French Revolution, the national manufactories established under royal patronage fell into swift decline, and to stimulate their regeneration the Marquis d'Avèze was appointed Commissioner of National Manufactures in 1797. In the same year he organized a national exhibition to display French manufactures to the world. Further 'Expositions of the Products of National Industry' were thereafter held intermittently, but from 1839, were organized on a regular quinquennial basis. Many other countries sought to emulate their undoubted success as a government-sponsored shop-window for national products. The Great Exhibition of 1851 broadened the scope to an international scale, and there followed a succession of similar events in every corner of the globe.

The element of national rivalry in international exhibitions was always prominent, and the trend towards using design as a means of both enhancing trading potential and asserting national prestige became more pronounced in the twentieth century. Governmental support and intervention became more politically assertive in the inter-war years, culminating in the Paris International Exposition of 1937, which was physically dominated by the 158–9 two giant pavilions of Germany and the Soviet Union confronting each other across a main entrance. Both countries included large numbers of industrial goods as part of their attempts to demonstrate the superiority of their system to a large international audience, the number of prizes awarded to them being trumpeted as an indication of national supremacy.

158–9 In both the German (left) and Soviet (above) pavilions at the 1937 Paris International Exposition, industrial products were displayed as symbols of national prestige, though providing a strong contrast in each case with the pompous interior decorations

Exhibitions could also be used an an instrument for internal political education and propaganda. During and after the Second World War, many were organized by the British government on an extensive range of subjects. A major exhibition took place in London in 1946 under the title 'Britain Can Make It', designed by James Gardner. The overall theme was 'swords into ploughshares', showing how war industries could be turned to peaceful uses. One stand showed, for example, the aluminium frame of an aircraft being converted into saucepans. The exhibition was bright and colourful, and a notable feature was the stress placed on the role of design in creating a hopeful vision of the future. In that sense, it was undoubtedly successful. Unfortunately, the majority of the goods on show were either for export only, or were in a prototype stage and not generally available. This obvious disparity led to the exhibition being dubbed, 'Britain Can't Have It', an example of propagandistic intent rebounding on a government when it aroused expectations it could not satisfy.

Between the two world wars, competitions of various kinds became the focus of national prestige, with races and record-breaking attempts for aircraft and cars receiving extensive government funding and support. The Schneider Trophy races for float-planes between 1919 and 1931 were one of the most notable air competitions of the period, arousing tremendous public interest. The race began as a sporting contest, the trophy to be awarded to the first country winning a total of three races. However, after the Italian Fascist party came to power in 1923, its leader, Mussolini, set out to demonstrate his country's regeneration by all means available, and ordered the aircraft-manufacturing company Macchi to win the trophy 'at all costs'. This challenge was acknowledged in other countries. In 1926 the Macchi M39, a low-wing monoplane with very clean aerodynamic lines, was victorious in a race notable for the fact that all the competing teams were government-subsidized, and all the pilots military. In subsequent years, competition continued to be intense, and the tempo of technical development accelerated as the participating nations strove for superiority. There was little doubt that competition of this type could force the pace of development by concentrating attention and resources. In 1931 the trophy was finally won 160 outright for Britain by the Supermarine S6B designed by R.J. Mitchell, who later emerged as a decisive figure in the development of British fighter-aircraft in the inter-war years.

In the Schneider Trophy races, the early, somewhat awkward sea-planes were replaced by streamlined monoplane racers, a form first introduced by the Americans and well exemplified by the S6B, its powerful aerodynamic lines setting the pattern for subsequent aircraft-design in Britain. The horizontal corrugations on the fuselage were part of the oil-cooling system,

160 Supermarine S6B floatplane, with signatures of the victorious Schneider Trophy team

but also provided a strong linear visual emphasis, a device frequently adopted for decorative purposes when streamlining became fashionable.

In the Soviet Union, too, there was awareness of the prestige value of air-records, but in the 1930s size became the dominant feature, the grandiose character of Stalinist architecture being mirrored in a series of gigantic craft, culminating in the *Maxim Gorky* of 1934, a huge eight-engined passenger-liner with a wing-span some twenty-five metres wider than that of a present-day Boeing 747 'Jumbo' liner. The form of the craft was bulky, depending on mass and weight rather than visual co-ordination for its effect. It required a crew of twenty to operate it, carried eighty passengers, and had a newspaper office with a two-colour printing press in one wing, and a photographic dark-room in the other, with loudspeakers and lights under the wings to broadcast or flash slogans to the population over which it flew. On a demonstration flight, however, an accompanying fighter went out of

187

161 The airship *Graf Zeppelin* over a Hitler Youth rally at Nuremberg

control when performing aerobatics, and hit the *Maxim Gorky* which crashed with heavy loss of life.

The dramatic form of airships was very suitable for propaganda purposes, though here, too, efforts could be spectacularly counter-productive. When the National Socialists came to power in Germany in 1933, giant Zeppelins *161* were used to hover over party rallies or follow Hitler's triumphal processions through cities, but the funeral pyre of the airship *Hindenburg* after an explosion while docking at Lakenhurst, New Jersey, at the end of a transatlantic voyage in 1937, marked the end of such exercises.

A similarly disastrous fate befell the British government's involvement in airship design. In 1923 it was proposed to use airships for passenger services on the imperial route between England and India. The political and strategic value of the link was stressed, but national prestige was also invoked, particularly the need to challenge German supremacy in this field. The scale of such craft, and the interest their massive torpedo-shaped forms provoked wherever they appeared, made them a valuable image of technical achievement at a time when the conquest of the air was still sufficiently recent to be awesome and exciting. However, since the Labour government then in power did not wish a private company to have a monopoly in construction, two prototypes were commissioned, one from Vickers, with a team under Dr Barnes Wallis, and another from a government engineering team. The Vickers' craft, R100, successfully completed a transatlantic crossing to Canada and back, but the second, the R101, was rushed to completion on the orders of the Air Minister, Lord Thompson of Cardington, who planned to use it on its maiden voyage for a visit to India in late 1930. Despite its known defects, prestige was placed before airworthiness, and the R101 crashed at Beauvais in northern France, only a fraction of its journey completed, with Lord Thompson among the dead. The recriminatory debate that ensued over the tragedy centred on an interpretation of the respective merits of 'private' and 'socialist' design and construction, the success of the R100 being seen as a vindication of the former.

A similar ideological interpretation was applied to the design development of the Supermarine Spitfire, which first flew in 1936, *162* becoming famous as a mainstay of the Royal Air Force in the Second World War. The Spitfire was a superb and beautiful fighter-plane, designed by R.J. Mitchell on the basis of his experience in the Schneider Trophy series. There can be no doubting his technical ability or his feel for fine graceful lines, but popular depiction of his achievement as representing the triumph of an inspired individual over the bumbling interference of civil servants was subsequently corrected by Jeffrey Quill, Supermarine's chief test pilot in the development phase of the Spitfire. In a letter to *Flight* magazine in 1974 he wrote that 'there existed a very close personal relationship between the designers in industry, the Air Staff and the government establishments'. He expanded on this theme at a 'Mitchell Memorial Symposium' held in 1976. 'The prototype was designed to Air Ministry Specification F.37/34 for a day and night fighter. It was not – as legend sometimes has it – a private venture; its design and construction were covered by Air Ministry Contract. There had, however, been private venture work involved in the early project design stages.' On the basis of Quill's evidence and personal experience, the success of the project seemed to have been based on close co-operation and mutual respect between government officials and the Supermarine team.

The example of the Spitfire highlights what is undoubtedly the most vitally important function of industrial design in political terms, that is, its decisive role in the establishment of military superiority. It is a predominant feature of our present age, unpalatable but unavoidable, that war and arms-

162 R.J. Mitchell's Supermarine Spitfire which first flew in 1936

races have been a major catalytic instrument of both material and social change, stimulating a pace and range of development that has had effects far beyond the military sphere.

Although war acts as a stimulus to design, the effectiveness of innovation is heavily conditioned by military attitudes. The outbreak of the First World War, for example, presented military leaders with problems they had difficulty in comprehending. The predominant response to the stalemate of trench-warfare on the Western Front was to use artillery concentrations and human-wave attacks to bludgeon a way through and re-establish the traditional pattern of fluid, cavalry-led war. The development of armoured tanks by the British in 1917 could have been decisive; however, the machines were misapplied. They were introduced in a sector where deep mud and a terrain pitted by gunfire nullified their speed and manoeuvrability.

Early tanks had a heavy lozenge-shaped appearance, but as designs for tanks and armoured vehicles proliferated in the inter-war period, military emphasis on functionalism resulted in a predominance of simple geometric *164* elements – an irony given the widespread equation of such forms with humanistic values. The use of heavy armoured plate, which was less susceptible to shaping, in sections of flat sheet, gave many of these vehicles a *163* faceted angularity, as in the German Mark IV tank, produced continuously throughout the Second World War, which created a daunting impression of destructive might and brutal efficiency. The aesthetics of fear are rarely discussed, or even acknowledged, yet the powerful impersonal forms of military weaponry are among the most widespread and evocative images of our age.

190

The search for naval supremacy has also prompted many design innovations. The century began with a race between Britain and Germany to gain numerical advantage in improved types of conventional vessels such as heavy battleships. The development of submarines as an effective instrument of warfare, however, and their use in numbers in both world wars by the German Navy for attacks on seaborne supplies, twice brought Britain to the

163–4 The forbidding angularity of Second World War armoured vehicles: (above) German Mark IVG tank; (below) British Humber armoured car

165 The organic form of the nuclear-powered USS *Ray* is the manifestation of a functional harmony with its natural element that contrasts strongly with its destructive capacity

verge of defeat. The hydrodynamic form of First World War U-boats was an important influence on concepts of streamlining, and the use of new forms of propulsion – heavy electric motors when submerged, and diesel engines for surface use – had widespread civil application in the post-war years. Submarines have since become a central element of naval strategy, the streamlined purity of form in vessels such as the nuclear-powered USS *Skipjack* of 1958 and its successors presenting a stark counterpoint to the 165 destructive potential of their nuclear missiles. In the knowledge of its annihilative power, it might seem inappropriate to speak of it in aesthetic terms, yet in its element it has, in W. B. Yeats' phrase, 'a terrible beauty'.

The problems of discussing design values in relation to military and political purposes are nowhere more evident than when one considers Germany in the period of the Third Reich. The memory of a regime that applied the principles of industrial rationalization to the extermination of millions of human beings is still hauntingly strong, and understandably, historians have frequently eschewed consideration of design in that context. Yet design values were extensively used by the Nazi regime for the furtherance of their policies, and for ideological justification and propaganda.

The ways in which design was used were varied, but underlying them all was the progressive harnessing of the resources of the nation and economy for the purposes of an aggressive, expansionist foreign policy. From 1935 onwards, an ever-greater emphasis was placed on a policy of autarky, of increasing the level of national economic self-sufficiency. This required the extended application of materials readily produced within Germany, notably light metals such as aluminium and magnesium, plastics and native timber products, as substitutes for imports. The effect on design was evident in two broad trends that in formal terms appear contradictory, but had common ground in the policy just described. The first was a sophisticated technical modernity, necessary to provide the requisite material superiority in weapons and equipment for the fulfilment of Hitler's expansionist aims. Innovation and quality in design and production were constantly stressed, and the aesthetics of goods and mechanisms were emphasized as a visible manifestation of German superiority. Exhibitions of 'Art and Technology' were frequent, and an official journal for engineers and technologists, *Deutsche Technik*, included a regular feature, 'The Beauty of Technology', with high-standard photographs of, for example, the latest Siemens' electrical equipment, or details of a Messerschmitt 109, emphasizing the 166 often compelling excellence of the visual form. In 1938, the German Prize, Hitler's answer to the Nobel Prize, was jointly awarded to four engineer-designers: Ferdinand Porsche of Volkswagen fame; Fritz Todt, head of the

166 Siemens' electrical instruments used as an example of the 'beauty of technology' in the journal *Deutsche Technik*, 1939

organization that built autobahns; and the aircraft designers Ernst Heinkel and Wilhelm Messerschmitt, for their 'cultural work' and 'artistic creations'. The emphasis on visual form served a general propaganda purpose, but it is noticeable that the military applications and capabilities of designs were rarely mentioned, aesthetics being used as an instrument to disguise real goals, while at the same time glorifying the means of attaining them.

The second, contrasting, trend emphasized traditional values and forms, with the German variants of the Arts and Crafts movement linked to 'blood and soil' ideology, and the virtues of time-honoured forms made from German materials contrasted with the 'rootless cosmopolitanism' of 1920s, functional design. Many traditional types of furniture, such as chairs in forms similar to the Anglo-American Windsor type, were produced in large quantities, to unified specifications, for use in public settings such as autobahn restaurants and factory-canteens. Standardized designs such as *167–8* those for the 'Beauty of Labour' organization, intended for factories, offices and worker settlements, provided a combination of economic advantage and nationalistic styling, in pursuit of a policy of allaying workers' discontents by means of environmental improvements.

In fact, the National Socialist regime used aesthetics on every possible occasion, and at all levels of life, as a propaganda instrument for cultural legitimization, and to secure suspension of rational judgment. One is faced

167–8 Traditional chair forms designed to standard specifications for the 'Schönheit der Arbeit' (Beauty of Labour) organization, 1937

169–70 Hawker
Hurricane (above)
designed by Sidney
Camm, and Me 109
(below) designed by
Wilhelm Messerschmitt

with the paradox that the standard of much industrial design is exceedingly high in this period, judged by accepted criteria such as the relationship of materials to production processes, production quality and aesthetic form, yet the policies for which it was used were appalling in their goals and consequences. Those criteria of judgment are not necessarily invalidated by this fact, but it does mean that 'good design', however defined in terms specific to an artefact or mechanism, cannot automatically be associated with beneficial ethical or political ideals; such juxtapositions are frequent but do not constitute an equation.

Notwithstanding subjective national responses, if a comparison is made of design in Germany and Britain during this period, it is clear that in key areas, in both technical and formal respects, there were considerable similarities, as with the Hawker Hurricane and the Messerschmitt Me 109. Differences *169–70* between these two aircraft are discernible, but they are of detail rather than

171 Living-room furnished with 'Utility' furniture from the inaugural display, 1942

principle. Both countries required heavy goods locomotives for transporting military supplies, producing 'Austerity' designs intended to be simple in construction, and easy to manufacture and maintain. The urgency of the military requirements that stimulated their design resulted in similar forms that were austere and plain, with no concessions to presentation and appearance. The Arts and Crafts tradition, strong in both Britain and Germany, was pressed into service by the Board of Trade for a wartime programme of 'Utility' furniture. From 1942 onwards, a team under Gordon Russell adapted a limited series of traditional timber forms to industrial mass-production to provide basic furniture for 'bombees', people whose homes had been destroyed by bombing, and for newly-weds. Many other examples could be cited in the same vein. To a considerable extent, the common features of design in Germany and Britain can be attributed to broadly similar responses to the functional demands of military operations. Similarities in the repertoire of forms and their functional capabilities do not imply, however, that the political philosophies and social aims of the combatant countries were identical.

America's entry into the war, and the harnessing of its productive might and design-capability to the manufacture of weapons and materials, provided a decisive and overwhelming material superiority, well illustrated by the way the American automobile industry turned from highly styled consumer products to functional vehicles, such as the Willys Jeep of which over half a million were produced by the end of the war. Its rugged form reflected the process of stripping the automobile to absolute essentials, which at the same time made it adaptable to a variety of functions. It was cited by General Eisenhower as one of the four instruments that most contributed to the Allied victory (the others being the DC-3, the 'bazooka' anti-tank gun and the nuclear bomb). Though the Jeep's comfort and stability were less than admirable, its sturdiness and versatility in all conditions and terrains were excellent. It was adapted after the war for use in farm-work and rural conditions, establishing a new concept of functional form for such vehicles that has been widely emulated, the British 'Land-Rover' being one of the most consistently successful designs. *172–3*

It seemed during the war that few areas of production in America were incapable of being transformed by mass-production methods, with aircraft, vehicles and weapons flowing in endless streams from assembly lines. One of *174* the most dramatic areas was shipbuilding, in which automobile construction methods were applied to 'Liberty' ships, standardized cargo vessels based on the time-proven form of the British tramp-steamer. Over sixty per cent of the vessel was prefabricated, entire sections such as living quarters complete with all fittings, bunks, washbasins and heating, simply being swung into place and welded on. The original estimated construction time was four and a half months, but this was drastically cut, the vessel *Robert E. Peary* being completed in November 1942 in just over four and a half days, and going into service three days later. In a laconic statement that typified the American approach to war-production, the administrator of the programme, Admiral Land, commented in 1943: 'The Liberty ship is a product for war use. It can be classed with the tank, the fighting planes and other materials of war. It was produced to be expendable if necessary. If expended, it had served its purpose.'

In contrast, the German approach to military design emphasized quality and durability, in an attempt to counter America's mass-production capacity. The problem, however, was that German weaponry and equipment, however good, could not be replaced when destroyed at the same rate as the Americans', who also demonstrated that mass-production did not necessarily imply inferior standards. The 'throw-away' concept has, with much justification, frequently been criticized, but it would be difficult to deny that in the context of the war, it had its virtues; a further example, in fact, of the way in which changed political or social circumstances can alter the perception of, and values attributed to, designs.

172–3 The Willys Jeep on display and under working conditions. It remains one of
the most enduring images of the Second World War

174 Nose-sections of B29 bombers on the assembly line of Boeing's plant at Wichita, Kansas, 1944

Since the end of the Second World War, the involvement of governments in weapons research and design has continued unabated, and has been extended, especially in the USA and the Soviet Union, to space-exploration, which by the late 1960s provided a new range of stylistic elements based on the forms of rockets, space modules and their equipment, that have been widely applied to static, mundane objects, much as streamlining was adopted as a purely stylistic device in the 1930s.

The main direction of government policies, however, is to more terrestrial concerns, and particularly to fostering design as a commercial aid. Bodies such as the Council of Industrial Design, founded in Britain in 1944, have been established to stimulate interest in and improvement of design in industry, especially in export trades. Even in the Soviet Union, where commercial competition and consumer orientation were lacking as stimuli to industrial design, the need to export and compete in international markets led in 1962 to the foundation of the All-Union Scientific Research Council for Industrial Design, under Yuri Soloviev. In Japan, the Ministry of Trade and Industry runs an Industrial Arts Institute, providing design services for small manufacturers, and an industrial products-checking laboratory that tests and proves all products for export.

Political influence on design is revealed in diverse ways, some overt and clearly apparent, others more oblique; though forms are rarely a unique reflection or expression of particular policies or ideologies. The exercise of political influence has been facilitated by the development of designing as an activity limited in its range of considerations, without control over the preconditions or applications of its specialist work. Within this framework of limitations, designers retain a measure of autonomy, their work determined not only by social and economic relationships and political decisions, but also by personal factors such as inherent talent and individual relationships. Forms of outstanding aesthetic and functional quality may therefore be attained under the most inauspicious circumstances, and to evaluate designs in terms of the purpose for which they are applied need not imply a denial or rejection of the creative capacity that shaped them. However, whether the innate power of human creativity embodied in the manifold works of designers is used for beneficial and life-enhancing purposes, or for repression and destruction, has become dependent to an ever-increasing degree on decisions taken by governmental bodies, and there is little sign of this determining role of political institutions being diminished.

Conclusion

In the course of its historical development, the role of industrial design has focused on making technology usable in forms that are accessible and comprehensible to the greatest possible number of people. Design has become a specialized activity in the industrial division of labour, one of a number of activities clustered under the general title of 'research and development', in which the creative activities associated with inventing and defining forms have become separated from the work-processes by which they are realized.

For the most part, designers have accepted and accommodated themselves to this specialized, organizational role, seeing their work as an autonomous activity concerned with refining and advancing defined forms and functions. It would be totally unjust, however, to depict designers simply as institutional functionaries. There can be found in their ranks a high proportion of socially aware and responsible men and women, sensitive to the needs not only of those who employ them, but of those who use and are affected by the forms they design. Their work has in large measure contributed to the improved health, comfort and convenience that are accepted as part of the normal life of an increasing proportion of the human race, and represent a standard of aspiration for those to whom they are not available.

Yet the growing industrial design profession finds itself enmeshed in a complex web of problems. That it operates within organizational and institutional constraints, determined and controlled by the policy decisions of people not always socially accountable for their consequences, is in itself a source of disquiet. Technical progress and excellence of design, in inward-looking terms, can no longer be considered unconditionally beneficial in a world increasingly beset by problems of enormous dimensions, such as the depletion of finite material resources, the increase of environmental pollution, the degradation of the nature of work by mechanization or the displacement of workers by automation, and the gulf between the 'haves' of the industrial countries, and the 'have-nots' of the so-called 'under-developed countries'.

The problems can be illustrated at various levels. The Anglo-French Concorde airliner, for example, is a superb technological achievement and

176   one of the most outstandingly beautiful forms of our time. The curved flow of its delta-wing and the sharp angle of the adjustable nose-configuration create an awesome bird-like image. Yet its enormous development cost and the environmental problems associated with its operation cannot be ignored.

175   In 1978 Fiat of Italy produced a new car, the 'Ritmo', on an automated production line, and advertised it as being 'Handbuilt by robots'. The design is excellent, but the social problems of unemployment created by such production methods are not easily solved. Even small items of manufacture can have a cumulative effect that exemplifies these problems. Pens, for instance, were originally made from goose-quills, a renewable natural resource. The Parker 51 fountain pen of 1939, designed by a team under Kenneth Parker, though expensive, was extremely efficient and, with its rolled-gold cap and arrow-shaped clip, a distinctive status-symbol. In the 1950s efficient ball-point and felt-tip pens, often of pleasing design, became cheaply available on a massive scale; yet beside this obvious social benefit must be set the dependence of plastic production on non-renewable petroleum resources, and the problems of waste-disposal represented by the millions of such objects at the end of their limited useful lives. There is an increasing conflict between most people's interests as consumers, for example as owners of private transport, and their social and environmental concerns.

Many designers are conscious of their social responsibilities and have sought to apply their skills and creativity to meeting long-term or minority needs, not served by giant corporations catering for mass-markets. Such

175 Fiat 'Ritmo' production line

176 BAC/SAC Concorde airliner in landing/take-off configuration

work has sometimes been possible in a commercial context, as where smaller, specialist firms have become aware of the contribution designers can make to their products. The German medical equipment firm Erbe of Tübingen, for example, commissioned Tomàs Maldonado together with Gui Bonsieppe and Rudolf Scharfenberg to design a range of electronic surgical and radiation equipment in which concepts of standardization developed in the mass-production of consumer goods were applied to a set of microwave radiation units to make them easier to produce, and more effective and flexible in use.

177–8

Non-commercial design research has been funded by many public and private institutions. The Nuffield Trust in Britain published *Studies in the Functions and Design of Hospitals*, 1955, which identified many deficiencies, and in 1961 provided funds for a research team, under L. Bruce Archer and

Misha Black at the Royal College of Art, to investigate the design of non-surgical hospital equipment. A hospital-bed of adjustable height, angle and profile was designed to ensure the comfort of patients and facilitate nursing.

Projects to alleviate suffering and poverty in economically under-developed countries have also engaged many designers, although these have sometimes run into unforeseen difficulties. In 1955 the International Co-operation Administration, a division of the US State Department, commissioned five leading design agencies to provide technical assistance for small manual industries in the Far and Middle East and Latin America. Russel Wright, who eventually abandoned commercial work and became deeply involved in the programme, wrote that: 'In design, we will advise according to traditional motifs what products might be developed for a wider area. . . . We will never "hot-house" industries which never existed, but try to point out how a native craft can produce more efficiently and market more profitably.' Despite this sensitivity, the very criteria of efficiency and profitability and the fact that the larger markets envisaged were in the United States, introduced alien elements, and created an economic dependence that could not but harm indigenous cultural traditions.

Gui Bonsieppe, a former teacher at Ulm who subsequently worked in Chile and Brazil, highlighted the problems of industrial design in relation to 'dependent countries' in a paper to an international symposium, 'Design for

177–8 Erbetherm long-wave radiation instrument, 1931 (below), and the 12–240 Microwave Therapy Unit, designed by Tomàs Maldonado, 1961 (right)

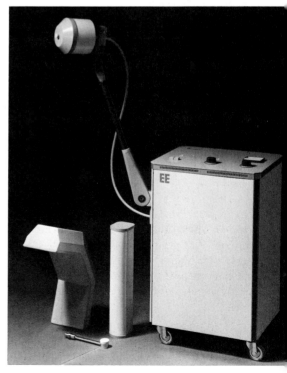

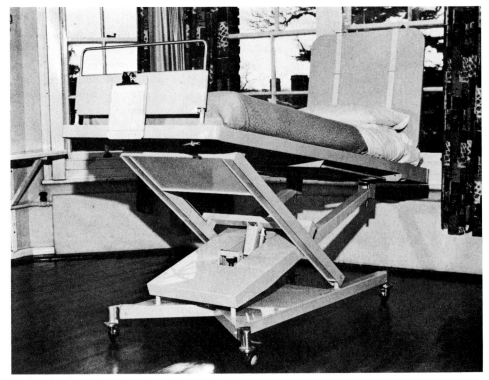

179 The Royal College of Art team researching hospital-bed design represented many disciplines, illustrating the co-operative nature of much of modern industrial design. The bed used a hydraulic jack as means of varying the configuration. Kenneth Agnew was the designer principally responsible for the final specification

Need', held at the Royal College of Art in London in 1976. He emphasized the lack of effective economic demand of the mass of population in these countries, and the need to 'make survival possible, to provide a life-support structure'. What was needed was not design *for* dependent countries, argued Bonsieppe, but design in and by dependent countries, on the basis of social need.

Other designers, foreseeing the end of industrialization as we know it, have explored the possibilities of 'alternative technology', using renewable resources such as solar energy, wind- and water-power, and applying natural materials to basic human needs such as shelter, warmth and food. At the extreme, Victor Papanek in his book *Design for the Real World*, 1971, castigated the industrial design profession in America for having 'elected to serve as pimp for big-business interests'. His condemnation of design for obsolescence as concerned more with inducing transient wants than fulfilling permanent needs, was at times barbed and accurate; but his stance became a total rejection of the capitalist economic system and the role of design within it, denying any virtue or beneficial effect whatsoever to either.

Papanek was influenced by the American architect and designer Buckminster Fuller, whose ideas on the social role of design have a comprehensiveness that is remarkable and rare. Fuller advocated imaginatively utilizing, rather than fearfully resisting, the potential for change in modern technology. Many of his designs have embraced technology with brilliant success, like his Dymaxion House project, begun in 1927, which was a total re-evaluation of living-space and domestic form.

Yet Fuller's technocratic vision, shared by Papanek, of designers as 'Comprehensive Anticipatory Design Scientists' – universal social and moral prophets of human survival and regeneration, transforming not only the environment, but the very nature of man – can appear more frightening in prospect than the political and ideological status quo it proposes to replace. There is little evidence to suggest that designers are any less subject to frailty and error, or any better suited to effecting such a transformation than any other group.

The concept of 'intermediate technology', on the other hand, popularized by Eugene Schumacher in the 1960s, is more modest in scope, accepting much of the rationale of modern technology, but seeking to apply it to problems of creating work and meaningful activity, rather than to concepts of efficiency and increased output that displace workers. Its emphasis is on the needs of people, rather than products. These ideas have found a response in under-developed countries doubtful of the benefits to them of technological progress on Western industrial lines. In India, the Ministry of Industrial Development established an Appropriate Technology Cell to explore the possibilities of techniques that were a development of traditional methods, expanding employment rather than reducing it.

In the industrialized countries there have been efforts to make design more responsive to social needs by developing new principles and methods. Methods of systematizing the process of design emerged in the 1960s, most notably in the work of Maldonado and a group of colleagues at Ulm, and of L. Bruce Archer and Christopher Jones in Britain. They proposed a rational analytical sequence intended to identify the fundamental nature of any given design problem, enabling a solution to be devised to meet defined needs, rather than to provide aesthetic refinement or stylistic innovation. Such problem-solving methodologies have had considerable influence on design-education and practice. While valuable in analysing complex requirements and establishing the parameters of design problems, they are less convincing

1.
THUD

2.

THE NEWEST
prefabricated bathroom
IS ALSO NEAREST

On the 29th floor of 40 Wall St. there sits the finished model of a new plumbing fixture that might well bug the eyes of any bystanding master plumber, a fixture that to all intents and purposes constitutes a one-piece bathroom. Designed by Architect Buckmister Fuller (Dymaxion House, Dymaxion Car) it accomplishes, by the simple connection of four basic parts, a complete bathroom weighing 404 pounds, with integral lavatory, toilet and bath. First known as the "Five by Five" (because that's the space it takes up), the official designation is now "The Integrated Bath".

In the research department of the Phelps Dodge Corporation it sits, ready for moderate production (100 units) in 1937. Architect Fuller has assigned his patents to the PD organization, and rumor discerns a new manufacturing and marketing subsidiary in the immediate offing. The range of uses for the unit is broad: pullmans, planes, trailers, trains, but mainly small homes. In fact, Mr. Fuller hopes this light, compact, complete bathroom will even inspire renters to install copies in their apartments, and remove them when they move. All of which lies in the realm of speculation. For the immediate future the device will probably induce fewer orders than conversations. None the less the fact remains that this prefabricated bathroom comes closer to commercial reality than any of its predecessors.

The Integrated Bathroom consists roughly of two oblong sections that form a partition where they join, which conceals the piping and other mechanical appurtenances. The sections (each

4.
PRESTO!

CLICK

SNAP
3.

a monometal stamping) are each split in the middle, the top being aluminum and the bottom 272 pounds of sheet copper unmetallized and tinted by a coating of silver, tin and antimony alloy. The bottom of one section is the lavatory and toilet, of the other a flat-bottomed tub.

The toilet, though reminiscent of the old backyard one-holer, is fully sanitary. The seat lifts and, remains upright by compression against the walls. Underneath is a standard form of bowl (though chrome nickel bowls are also available).

Two men can handle an installation in three hours, for all piping except a minimum amount of connection material is integral with the unit. So are electric connections, ventilation equipment, etc. Fresh air is drawn by a motor under the lavatory from the nearest room, and exhausted wherever circumstances permit.

Miscellaneous features: A composition Venetian blind gives privacy to the bather, and, while permitting the escape of steam, prevents the escape of water. The door frame between the two sections is six inches thick, permitting use as seat. Complete cleansing of tub is easily attained. The plumbing layout was devised in collaboration with a local master plumber, copper tubing being used for water lines. Particular care was used to avoid back-siphonage possibilities. Sliding doors conserve space. The metallic finish has a "hammered" appearance while at the same time being thoroughly sanitary, the inventor claims. Under surfaces of the base metal are covered with Dumdum, a sound deadening material. An electric heating system between the two units warms the metal itself, radiating heat to occupant of bathroom. Removable panels permit access to plumbing traps and connections under toilet and lavatory.

180 Buckminster Fuller's Dymaxion Bathroom, as advertised in *The Ladle*, 1937

at the point where a solution is given shape. For many designers, rational analysis alone is too deterministic and impersonal; an intuitive synthesis and instinctive feeling for 'rightness' in form is regarded as necessary to ensure individuality of expression and a vital human element in design.

Despite industrial designers' efforts to find new directions and roles, most will continue to work for industrial or governmental organizations within existing economic and social structures. Many of these organizations employ research groups numbering thousands, including numerous designers, who are working at the frontiers of technology in fields such as micro-electronics and automation. There is little doubt that commercial imperatives will result in designers giving form to many new materials, processes and mechanisms that are capable of making a significant contribution to solving crucial social problems. Whether this contribution will be made, and who will benefit, are questions beyond the powers of designers alone to answer. In this respect, they have no more and no less responsibility than any other citizens. The answers to such questions, however, will condition the purposes design will serve and the role it will play for the future.

The immediate future has already been shaped in the offices, studios and workshops of countless industrial designers across the world. The time-lag between the conception of a design and its appearance in marketable form often extends to several years, and means that much of what is seen as new today is already a part of design history.

Despite the flood of new products, and built-in obsolescence, countless time-honoured designs remain in widespread production and use, satisfying continuing needs or being adapted to purposes their creators never imagined. Many historical designs of all kinds have been preserved by collectors or museums increasingly aware of their value as visible reminders of the patterns of everyday life in the past. Yet the vast majority of items of former daily use have been destroyed, recycled, or buried in waste-tips, the tumuli of our material culture, to await the attention of future generations of industrial archaeologists. It is a history that has as yet been only partially explored, but provides tangible evidence of an incredible wealth of human achievement, as rich and diverse as the range of motives, tastes and desires that inspired it. There can be few people in industrialized countries, moreover, whose memories are not vividly alive with recollections of the sight, feel and sound of objects, implements and machines that have long since disappeared, but formed part of the fabric of their hardships, pleasures, achievements and aspirations. In this respect, everyone is a historian of industrial design.

Select bibliography

The only bibliography concentrating specifically on design is A.J. Coulson, *A Bibliography of Design in Britain*, 1979, which includes references to books and articles on the development of industrial design, not only in Britain, but also referring to key influences from other countries, though in this latter respect it makes no claim to completeness.

Ambasz, E., *Italy: The New Domestic Landscape*, New York, 1972. A catalogue of a wide-ranging Museum of Modern Art Exhibition on modern Italian design, containing essays on Italian design history and theory and many superb illustrations.

Ames, K.L., *Grand Rapids Furniture at the Time of the Centennial*, in I.M.G. Quimby, *Winterthur Portfolio 10*, Charlottesville, 1975. An excellent, detailed case-study.

Architectenkammer Hessen. Catalogue, *Ferdinand Kramer, Werkkatalog 1923–74*, Frankfurt, 1975. Contains a broad range of work by a leading member of the New Frankfurt movement.

Arts Council of Great Britain. Catalogue, *Art in Revolution* (Soviet Union), 1971. Contains references to avante-garde experiment. Catalogue, *The Thirties*, 1979, includes industrial designs, though the selection is unrepresentative.

Atterbury, P., and L. Irvine, *The Doulton Story*, London, 1979. An excellent small catalogue of the company's history and products.

Banham, P. Reyner, *Theory and Design in the First Machine Age*, London, 1960. An important work on early twentieth-century avant-garde movements in architecture and design.

Baroni, P., *Rietveld Furniture*, London, 1978. A detailed account with numerous drawings and illustrations.

Bayley, S., *In Good Shape*, London, 1979. Contains an interesting selection of texts, and a range of illustrations of modern design, though the author's view of design as the 'legitimate art' of the century is tendentious.

Baynes, K., *Industrial Design and the Community*, London, 1967. A brief account by a practising designer.

Beer, E.H., *Scandinavian Design: Objects of a Life Style*, New York, 1975. The best book to date on the artist-designers. Written with enthusiasm and beautifully illustrated.

Bell, Q., *The Schools of Design*, London, 1963. A scholarly account of the attempts to establish a system of design education in Britain in the nineteenth century.

Benton, T., *The New Objectivity*; T. and C. Benton, *Design 1920s*; T. Benton and others, *Europe 1900–1914*, Milton Keynes, 1975. A series of Open University texts on architecture and design that have made a major contribution to developing the study of the history of design. T. and C. Benton with Dennis Sharp, *Form and Function*, 1975. A wide-ranging anthology of selected texts.

Bertram, A., *Design*, Harmondsworth, 1938. A summary of 1930s reformist ideas attempting to educate the public to standards of 'good' design.

Bicknell, J., and L. McQuiston (eds.), *Design for Need*, Oxford, 1977. A series of papers given at the Royal College of Art conference of the same title.

Bishop, T. (ed.), *Design History: Fad or Function?*, London, 1978. Papers from the 1977 Design History Society conference with some good contributions on varied aspects of industrial design.

Bøe, A., *From Gothic Revival to Functional Form: A Study of Victorian Theories of Design*, Oslo, 1957. A detailed and scholarly work.

Buddensieg, T., and H. Rogge, *Industriekultur: Peter Behrens und die AEG*, Berlin, 1979. A first detailed account of Behrens' work for the company with an extensive catalogue of designs.

Bush, D., *The Streamlined Decade*, New York, 1975. A well illustrated study that did much to correct the neglect of this period of American design.

Campbell, J., *The German Werkbund: The Politics of Reform in the Applied Arts*, Princeton, 1978. Concentrates on the politics rather than visual aspects, but a valuable study of this subject.

Carrington, N., *Industrial Design in Britain*, London, 1976. A personal account that has a narrower scope than the title suggests.

Celant, G., *Marcello Nizzoli*, Milan, 1968. An Italian text, interesting for the illustrations of preparatory sketches as well as of finished work.

Dickinson, H.W., *Matthew Boulton*, Cambridge, 1936. A dated study but still useful.

Dickson, D., *Alternative Technology and the Politics of Technical Change*, London, 1974. A survey of modern alternatives to industrial society including a discussion of the implications for design.

Doblin, J., *One Hundred Great Product Designs*, New York, 1970. An interesting selection with comments by a noted American designer.

Dorfles, G., *Il Disegno Industriale e la sua Estetica*, Bologna, 1963. An introduction to the aesthetics of design by a leading Italian scholar and theorist.

Drexler, A., *Charles Eames: Furniture from the Design collection, the Museum of Modern Art*, New York, 1973. An illustrated collection of Eames' finest work.

Dreyfuss, H., *Designing for People*, New York, 1955. A genial and delightful account by one of the greatest of modern designers.

Dubois, J., *Plastics History USA*, Boston, 1972. A study of its development and diffusion.

Ellis, C.H., *The Lore of the Train*, London, 1971. A large tome on the development of locomotives and rolling stock in many lands. A good general introduction, profusely illustrated.

Farr, M., *Design in British Industry – A Mid-Century Survey*, Cambridge, 1955. An extensive survey but adopts a moral tone towards design.

Faulkner, T. (ed.), *Design 1900–1960: Studies in Design and Popular Culture of the 20th Century*, Newcastle, 1976. A collection of papers from the first conference on design history to be held in Britain.

Forty, A. and G. Newman, *British Design*, Milton Keynes, 1975. Another Open University text, with a good account of electrification in the home and its influence on design in Britain.

Fossati, P., *Il Design in Italia: 1945–1972*, Milan, 1973. Describes and illustrates the outstanding achievements of post-war Italian designers.

Geffrye Museum, London. Catalogue: *Utility Furniture and Fashion 1941–1951*, 1974. A short but excellent catalogue on the British government's intervention in design in the Second World War.

Gemeentemuseum, The Hague. Catalogue: *Piet Zwart*, The Hague, n.d. (*c.* 1976). Describes the evolution of Zwart's work in graphic and industrial design.

Giedion, S., *Mechanization takes Command*, New York, 1948. At times idiosyncratic, but an essential text, with a wealth of examples of mechanized products from all aspects of daily life.

Goodison, N., *Ormolu: the work of Matthew Boulton*, London, 1974. Although concentrating on a specialized aspect of Boulton's production the book contains excellent chapters on design and production at Soho.

Greif, M., *Depression Modern: The Thirties Style in America*, New York, 1975. A product of personal enthusiasm rather than scholarship, but well illustrated and conveying the flavour of the period.

Hald, A., and S.E. Skawonious, *Contemporary Scandinavian Design*, Leigh-on Sea, 1952. A somewhat dry account of the artist-designers' work.

Hard af Segerstad, U., *Modern Finnish Design*, London, 1968. A brief account of its evolution and leading figures.

Haresnape, B., *Railway Design since 1830* (two volumes), London, 1968, and *British Rail: A Journey by Design*, London, 1980. Together these form a comprehensive account of the changes in visual form on Britain's railways.

Holm, B. (ed.), *Funfzig Jahre Deutscher Normenausschuss*, Berlin, 1967. An official account of the development of standardization in Germany.

Hutchings, R., *Soviet Science, Technology, Design: interaction and convergence*, London, 1976. Contains an account of the emerging role of design in the Soviet Union.

Katz, S., *Plastics: Designs and Materials*, London, 1978. An extensive account of the development, properties and applications of this most ubiquitous of modern materials. Well illustrated.

Kelly, A., *The Story of Wedgwood*, London, 1930. Dated, but more comprehensive than many later studies.

Kouwenhoven, J., *Made in America*, New York, 1975. A broad account of the emergence and impact of the 'American system'.

Lancaster, M., *Electric Cooking, Heating, Cleaning, etc.*, London, 1914. A rare but invaluable account of product design in the early years of the century.

Le Corbusier, *Towards a New Architecture*, London, 1927 (paperback 1970). An indispensable text for an insight on the impact of industrial products on one of the century's leading architects and theorists.

Lifshey, E., *The Housewares Story*, Chicago, 1973. Produced by a trade association and emphasizing commercial growth, but extensively illustrated and very useful.

Lincoln, E., *The Electric Home*, New York, 1936. Gives a period flavour at a point when electric products were rapidly being adopted in America.

Loewy, R., *The Locomotive: Its Esthetics*, London and New York, 1937; *Never Leave Well Enough Alone*, Paris, 1963; and *Industrial Design*, New York, 1979. Together, these form a fascinating account of the work and ideas of one of the most flamboyant and successful modern designers.

MacCarthy, F., *All Things Bright and Beautiful*, London, 1972, revised as *A History of British Design, 1830–Today*, 1979. A partial view, concentrating on tendencies culminating in the foundation of the Council for Industrial Design.

Mana, J., *El Diseno industrial*, Barcelona, 1973. An excellent little book that shows a broad understanding of the historical evolution of design and an appreciation of it as a creative activity.

Meikle, J., *Twentieth Century Limited*, Philadelphia, 1979. A detailed account of the theory and practice of industrial design in the United States between the wars.

Meller, J., *The Buckminster Fuller Reader*, Harmondsworth, 1972. Fuller's writings are varied and extensive, but this anthology provides a good introduction.

Mercer, F. A., *The Industrial Design Consultant*, London and New York, 1947. A brief account at a point when consultancy work was developing in Britain.

Middleton, M., *Group Practice in Design*, London, 1967. An appreciation of group work that contains some good case studies.

Munari, B., *Design as Art*, Harmondsworth, 1971. One man's account of his transformation from artist to designer. A sometimes bizarre but fascinating book.

Neue Sammlung, Munich. Catalogue: *Zwischen Kunst und Industrie: der Deutsche Werkbund*, Munich, 1975. An extensive selection of texts and illustrations that chronicles the history of the Werkbund. Catalogue: *Wilhelm Wagenfeld: 30 jahre künstlerische mitarbeit in der industrie*, Munich, 1961. A well illustrated selection of work by one of Germany's leading designers.

Noblet, J. de, *Design*, Paris, 1974. Useful for its emphasis on French design, though its anthology and illustrations range much wider.

Olins, W., *The Corporate Personality*, London, 1978. An engaging account by a practitioner who knows the subject and its problems from the inside.

Papanek, V., *Design for the Real World*, New York, 1971 and London, 1972. Emphasizes the moral role of designers in a 'blueprint for human survival'.

Perry, J., *The Story of Standards*, New York, 1955. An account of the growth of standards in American industry.

Pevsner, N., *Pioneers of the Modern Movement*, London, 1936, revised as *Pioneers of Modern Design*, Harmondsworth, 1960. Itself a pioneering work, though focusing on the Modern Movement and its values to the exclusion of all else.

–, *An Enquiry into Industrial Art in England*, Cambridge, 1937. This study castigated ninety per cent of the industrial goods being produced in England on the grounds of standards of taste and morality that were altogether too lofty and lacking in understanding.

–, *Studies in Art, Architecture and Design* (two volumes), London, 1968. Contains some valuable essays on notable designers.

Pica, A., and others, *Forme Nuove in Italia*, Rome, 1957. An illustrated summary of trends in Italy in the 1950s.

Phillips, R. R., *The Servantless House*, London, 1920. Proposes mechanical appliances and various labour-saving devices as a remedy for the 'servant problem'.

Polak, A., *Glass, its makers and its public*, London, 1975. An excellent account of processes and their influence on form.

Rae, J., *The American Automobile*, Chicago, 1965. A standard account of the evolution of the automobile and its place in American life.

Read, H., *Art and Industry*, London, 1934. A profoundly influential work that pleaded for design to be created and viewed as abstract art.

Royal Academy, London. Catalogue: *50 Years Bauhaus*, 1968. A good summary of the institution, its personalities and its work.

Schaefer, H., *The Roots of Modern Design*, London, 1970. A well illustrated book that heavily emphasizes the functionalist strand of design history.

Selle, G., *Ideologie und Utopie des Designs*, Cologne, 1968. An effort to expound a theory of design as an expression of social relationships.

–, *Die Geschichte des Designs in Deutschland von 1870 bis heute*, Cologne, 1978. An excellent account of the social role of design in Germany.

Stavenov, A., and A. Huldt, *Design in Sweden*, Stockholm, 1961. A descriptive account of developments in Sweden that include industrial design.

Teague, W.D., *Design this Day*, New York, 1940 and London, 1947. A comprehensive statement of his ideas by one of the giant figures of American design.

Van Doren, H., *Industrial Design*, London and New York, 1954. Another account by a leading figure in the evolution of industrial design in 1930s America.

Wakefield, H., *Nineteenth Century British Glass*, London, 1961. A good account of continuity and change in this industry.

Wedgwood, Josiah and Sons Ltd. Catalogue: *Josiah Wedgwood: the Arts and Sciences United*, Barlaston, 1978. A small volume but aptly titled, showing the full range of Wedgwood's work and achievement.

White, J.H., Jr, *The American Railroad Passenger Car*, Baltimore, 1978. A huge and very detailed work, surely the definitive study of the subject.

Wilkins, B. (ed.), *Leisure in the Twentieth Century*, London, 1977. A further collection of papers from a conference of the Design History Society.

Wingler, H., *The Bauhaus*, Cambridge, Mass., 1969. A massively detailed volume covering all aspects of the institution.

Woodward, C.D., *The Story of Standards*, London, 1972. An official history of the British Standards Institution.

There is a very large range of journals of a general nature that contain material on design and products; the following is a short list of the most important specializing in design, with their dates of publication: in Britain, *Art and Industry*, 1936–1958, and *Design*, 1949–to date. In the USA, *Industrial Design*, 1954–to date, and *Design Quarterly*, 1946–to date. The latter is particularly useful for issues devoted to specific aspects of design and reviews of design in particular countries. In Italy, *Domus*, 1929–to date, and *Casabella*, 1928–to date. In France, *Art et Industrie*, 1925–to date, and *Design Industrie*, 1952–to date. The Swedish journal *Form*, 1905–to date, should not be confused with the German publication of the same title, *Form*, 1957–to date. In Switzerland *Das Werk* has been published continuously since 1915.

Acknowledgments

Illustrations have been reproduced by permission of the following: Firmenarchiv AEG-TELEFUNKEN, Brunswick 49–52; The American Museum in Britain, Bath 26; Archives Photographiques, Paris/ S.P.A.D.E.M. 158; Armouries, Her Majesty's Tower of London 32; Atlas Copco 140–3; A.T. & T. Co. Photo Center 84; Bauhaus-Archiv, Berlin 79; BBC Hulton Picture Library 171; Norman Bel Geddes Coll. at the Hoblitzelle Theatre Arts Library, Humanities Research Center, University of Texas at Austin, by permission of the executrix of the Norman Bel Geddes estate, Edith Lutyens Bel Geddes 86, 119; Berry Magicoal Ltd 120; Bibliothèque Royale, Brussels 66; Birmingham Museum and Art Gallery 1, 2, 11 (Museum of Science and Industry); Braun AG 116; British Airways 176; British Rail/Oxford Publishing Co. 19; The Budd Co. 104; Bundesarchiv, Koblenz 170; Canon, Inc. 149; Caravan Magazine 146; Chrysler Corporation 98; Collection Michael Collins 9; Irving Cooperman Collection 33; Corning Museum of Glass 28; Design Council of Great Britain 60, 132; Deutsches Museum, Munich 99; Deutsches Rundfunk-Museum, Berlin 135–7; Electrolux Ltd 124; Erbe Elektromedizin GmbH & Co. 178; Fiat 175; Fischer Fine Art, London 67; Ford Archives, Henry Ford Museum, Dearborn, Michigan 46–7, 53–5; Buckminster Fuller Archives 97, 180; Gemeente Musea, Amsterdam 75; General Motors Ltd 48, 154; Pictorial Coll., Grand Rapids Public Library 41; Haags Gemeentemuseum, The Hague 57; Hoover Ltd 123; IBM UK Ltd 115; Ideal-Standard Ltd 90, 91; Imperial War Museum, London 163–4, 172–4; Collection John Jesse 10; Kawasaki Heavy Industries Ltd 150–1; Kodak Museum 39–40, 82, 130; La Vie du Rail, Photo Grandgérard 103; London Transport Executive 109–10; From the Bert Love Collection 129; McDonnell Douglas Corporation 96; Minox GmbH 148; Montgomery Ward 43; Museum of British Road Transport, Coventry 23; Museum of Finnish Architecture, Helsinki 89; Museum of Modern Art, New York 80, 111–13; National Portrait Gallery, London 133; National Railway Museum, York 15–16, 106; Neue Galerie der Stadt Aachen, Sammlung Ludwig 147; Neue Sammlung, Munich 87; Nottingham Castle Museum 4; Oldsmobile Division, Lansing, Michigan 45; Olivetti 114, 118; Orrefors Glasbruk 93; Philips, Eindhoven 131; Pininfarina Archives 100; RAF Museum, Hendon 160, 162, 169; Revere Ware 127; Roneo Vickers Ltd 58; Royal Doulton Tableware Ltd 27, 68; Gordon Russell Ltd 92; Science Museum, London 12–14, 20, 35–8; Sears, Roebuck and Co. 42, 83; Sony Corporation of America 139; Süddeutscher Verlag 161; Gebrüder Thonet GmbH 24, 25; Tupperware Home Parties 128; US Navy 165; Universitätsbibliothek und Technische informations bibliothek, Hanover 59; Verkehrsmuseum, Nuremberg 101–2; Victoria and Albert Museum, London 7–8; Trustees of the Wedgwood Museum, Barlaston, Staffs. 3; West Point Museum, US Military Academy 31; Wilkinson Match Ltd 145; F. Wrighton & Sons Ltd 157

Index

Italic numbers refer to illustrations